M000211859

Tap into the Celtic ~~Mys~~

The ancient Celts believed that spirit inhabited all things, including the natural objects they used as divinatory tools. Though the druids often consulted omens and oracles to uncover hidden knowledge and foresee the future, no book before this one has focused solely on their divinatory practices.

Omens, Oghams & Oracles teaches skills you will use for the rest of your life for guidance and insight into any difficult problem or question. It offers specific directions and examples so that you can immediately use the various methods explained to achieve amazing results! Richard Webster presents the most practical and effective divinatory methods of the Celts plus two new variations that are particularly valuable for revealing information that may otherwise stay hidden.

These divination methods are easy to use and can be incorporated into any spiritual or magical system. Try them! They'll be just as useful to you as they were to the Celts. And you'll find that when you interpret the Celtic omens, oghams, and oracles, you receive insights rarely gained through other methods.

"[Omens, Oghams & Oracles] *will open your mind and spirit to new heights of awareness. Not only will you benefit, but in the true Druidic tradition, you will find yourself giving aid and comfort to others. Not since Scott Cunningham has a book made me want to stop whatever I was doing and immerse myself in another world and culture. Highly recommended!"*
 — *Carl Herron*
editor, The Path Review

"*Richard Webster has written a well-researched 'gem' for anyone interested in divination."*
 — *Dusty Cravens*
author of Runic Geomancy

About the Author

Richard Webster was born in Auckland, New Zealand, in 1946. New Zealand is still his home, though he travels widely every year lecturing and conducting workshops on psychic subjects around the world. He has written many books, mainly on psychic subjects, and also writes monthly columns for two magazines.

Richard began his working life in publishing and became in turn a bookstore proprietor, stage hypnotist, palmist, ghost writer, and magician before becoming a professional teacher and writer on psychic topics.

Richard is married with three children. His family is very supportive of the way Richard makes his living, but his older son, after watching his father's career, has decided to become an accountant.

To Write to the Author

If you wish to contact the author or would like more information about this book, please write to the author in care of Llewellyn Worldwide and we will forward your request. Both the author and publisher appreciate hearing from you and learning of your enjoyment of this book and how it has helped you. Llewellyn Worldwide cannot guarantee that every letter written to the author can be answered, but all will be forwarded. Please write to:

Richard Webster
c/o Llewellyn Worldwide
P.O. Box 64383-K800, St. Paul, MN 55164-0383, U.S.A.

Please enclose a self-addressed, stamped envelope for reply, or $1.00 to cover costs.
If outside U.S.A., enclose international postal reply coupon.

Free Catalog from Llewellyn

For more than 90 years Llewellyn has brought its readers knowledge in the fields of metaphysics and human potential. Learn about the newest books in spiritual guidance, natural healing, astrology, occult philosophy and more. Enjoy book reviews, new age articles, a calendar of events, plus current advertised products and services. To get your free copy of *Llewellyn's New Worlds of Mind and Spirit*, send your name and address to:

Llewellyn's New Worlds of Mind and Spirit
P.O. Box 64383-K800, St. Paul, MN 55164-0383, U.S.A.

Omens, Oghams & Oracles

Divination in the Druidic Tradition

Richard Webster

1995
Llewellyn Publications
St. Paul, Minnesota 55164–0383, U.S.A.

Omens, Oghams & Oracles. Copyright © 1995 by Richard Webster. All rights reserved. Printed in the United States of America. No part of this book may be used or reproduced in any manner whatsoever without written permission from Llewellyn Publications except in the case of brief quotations embodied in critical articles and reviews.

FIRST EDITION
First Printing, 1995

Cover design by Thomas Grewe
Cover illustrations by Carla Shale

Illustrations by Carla Shale
Editing, design, and layout by David Godwin

Library of Congress Cataloging in Publication Data

Webster, Richard, 1946–
    Omens, oghams, & oracles : divination in the druidic tradition /
Richard Webster. — 1st ed.
        p.   cm.
    Includes bibliographical references and index.
    ISBN 1–56718–800–1 (alk. paper)
    1. Divination.   2. Druids and Druidism.   3. Magic, Celtic.
I. Title.   II. Title: Omens, oghams, and oracles.
BF1770.G7W   1995
133.3'089'916—dc20   95–1559
                                                                        CIP

Llewellyn Publications
A Division of Llewellyn Worldwide, Ltd.
St. Paul, Minnesota 55164–0383, U.S.A.

Acknowledgments

I would like to thank all the people who have encouraged me, sometimes unknowingly, in this book: David and Penny Alexander, Dusty Cravens, Brian and Jan Flora, Carl Herron, Jon Kealoha, Charles Scott, and Donald Tyson. Grateful thanks to Max Maven for allowing me to use the term "druid sticks" that first appeared in his book *Max Maven's Book of Fortunetelling*. Special thanks to Carla Shale for her delightfully clear and helpful illustrations.

Other Books by Richard Webster

Freedom to Read (Auckland: HHP Press, 1972)
Your Tomorrowscope (Auckland: Brookfield Press, 1977)
Sun-Sign Success (Auckland: Brookfield Press, 1982)
The Stars and Your Destiny (Auckland: Brookfield Press, 1982)
How to Read Tea Leaves (Auckland: Brookfield Press, 1982)
Discovering Numerology (Auckland: Brookfield Press, 1983)
How to Read Minds (Auckland: Brookfield Press, 1984)
Secrets of Ghost Writing (London: Martin Breese, 1987)
How to Develop Your Psychic Power (London: Martin Breese, 1988)
Good Luck from Beijing (London: Martin Breese, 1990)
Revealing Hands (St. Paul: Llewellyn Publications, 1993)

Forthcoming

Talisman Magick

Dedication

To my American "family":
Brian, Jan, Ian, and Hillary Flora

Contents

Introduction

This book is really an account of an obsession I have had since 1967. In that year I visited Glastonbury for the first time. I was living in London that year and spent most weekends visiting historic, particularly holy, places. For some reason, it was many months before I was able to get to Glastonbury. I particularly wanted to get there because of its associations with King Arthur and the knights of the round table. I wandered around the abbey ruins thinking about what I had read of King Arthur, and what the abbey must have looked like when it was first built. It was a cool, windy, autumn day and the clouds formed strange patterns high above me. There were very few people visiting the abbey that day. As I walked I felt a sudden warmth around me and the abbey seemed to be completely rebuilt. My hands felt strangely warm and everything I looked at seemed colored with a special radiance. I felt completely revitalized and at peace with the entire world and everyone in it. It felt as if I belonged in this place and had been there hundreds of years earlier. Time stood still for me that day, and I was very late returning to London. The strange feeling of peace and belonging stayed with me for several days.

A few weeks later, I had similar feelings in Salisbury Cathedral. The feelings were much less intense, but were still strong. In the 1960s anyone could wander around Stonehenge, and the feelings were present there, also. It was several weeks before I mentioned my experiences to anyone. I was twenty years old at the time and was still cautious about discussing spiritual and psychic matters with others. I chose the right person to talk to. He suggested I return to Glastonbury Abbey and see if the feelings were still there on a return visit.

I had strange dreams for a few nights before visiting the abbey again. I was reluctant to go, because I was hoping that the feelings would return but was worried that they would not. I need not have been concerned. As soon as I entered the bounds of the original abbey, the sensation returned just as strongly and as powerfully as on the first visit.

I returned to London excited and thoughtful. I had watched the other visitors, and none had given any indication of receiving a mystical experience. My friend thought that perhaps I had had a partial recall of a past life. I gradually put the experience to the back of my mind.

Several months later, while living in Scotland, I heard about ley lines for the first time. I was intrigued to discover that Glastonbury, Salisbury, and Stonehenge were all interconnected. Glastonbury and Salisbury are, of course, important Christian centers of worship. A fascinating fact recorded by several researchers, including John Michell and Keith Critchlow, show that the dimensions and geometry of Stonehenge are duplicated in St. Mary's Chapel at Glastonbury, reputedly the first Christian chapel in England.

The position of Salisbury Cathedral was supposedly chosen by the flight of an arrow. However, in 1904 Francis J. Bennett showed that Salisbury Cathedral is on a direct line that goes from Stonehenge, through Old Sarum and Salisbury Cathedral to Clearbury Ring. The story of the arrow flight is a charming one, but obviously some other method must have been used to enable the cathedral to be built exactly on a ley line.

My fascination with all of this, coupled with my strong feelings at these ancient sites, led me quite accidentally into geomancy, the study of the earth's natural rhythms. One important

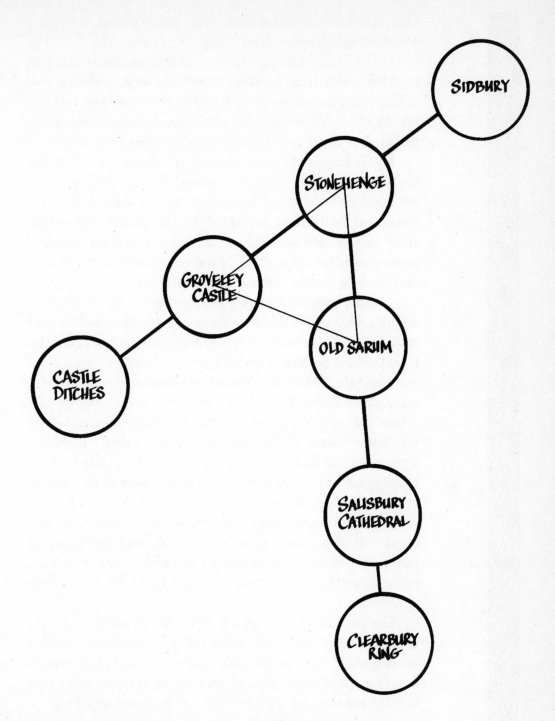

Ley Lines

aspect of this is divination, and I was quickly drawn on to learn about the oghams and druid sticks.

My landlady in Glasgow had a set of druid sticks that had been left behind by a previous boarder. The druid sticks are a set of four oblong sticks, each with one mark on one side and two on the other. When they are mixed in the hands and gently tossed, they create one of sixteen possible combinations.

My landlady and I experimented with these. It was a case of the blind leading the blind, but we had some startling successes. My landlady had lost touch with her brother some thirty years earlier and the druid sticks told her that she would be seeing him again soon. Weeks went by, and my landlady got disheartened. Several weeks later though, she answered a knock on the door to find her long-lost brother standing on the step.

Another instance I recall from this time is the druid sticks accurately telling me that I would be going to Cornwall for several months. This seemed most unlikely, but a month or so later I was living in Bodmin, Cornwall.

It was almost fifteen years before I came across anyone else using druid sticks. Since then I have met many other people scattered around the globe who use the druid sticks, including one "rune-master" in Albuquerque, Dusty Cravens, who at one time manufactured druid sticks. All of these people have encouraged me to write this book to enable these ancient arts to be utilized by people today.

The druid sticks naturally led me on to study the Celts and the druidic teachings. My experiments showed that many of their methods of divination are just as useful today as they were to the ancient Celts. Unfortunately, most people know very little about them.

The purpose of this book is to cover the more important methods of divination in the Celtic and druidic tradition that can be used today. Most of the book deals with forms of divination using wood and stones. The ogham fews and druid sticks are easy to make and use, and suitable stones can be found anywhere.

My enthusiasm for these various forms of divination is still as great as it was twenty-five years ago. I am sure you will become just as enthusiastic after you have tried them yourself.

CHAPTER ONE

The Celts

The Celts were Indo-Europeans who occupied the area north of the Black Sea by the source of the Danube. They can be traced back to the Early Bronze Age. About 2500 B.C. they began to spread across Europe and down towards India. By 300 B.C. they occupied all of Europe from the Baltic to the Mediterranean and from Britain to the Black Sea. It is believed that the first Celts arrived in Britain in 1472 B.C. Before them, there had been numerous arrivals of different people who successfully lived with the Stone Age Britons. The Celts made an impression with their knowledge of metalworking and their custom of burying their dead. They also had considerable road-building skills and were able to make roads through previously impenetrable forests. In fact, they were builders of roads well before the Romans. A Celtic road found preserved in a bog in 1985 was constructed on a foundation of oak beams, resting side by side on rails of oak, ash, and alder.[1]

The Celts were fearless fighters and were particularly renowned for their horsemanship. Both the Greeks and the Romans employed Celtic mercenaries. In his Gallic campaigns, Julius Caesar's horsemen were almost entirely Celts.[2]

The strength of the Celts was such that in 390 B.C. they successfully sacked Rome and withdrew only after payment of a massive fine. An attack on Delphi in 279 B.C. failed because of a freak fall of snow, which the Greeks attributed to their god Apollo. In 225 B.C. a huge army of Celts was defeated by the Romans in Telamon, marking the beginning of the end of Celtic supremacy. All the same, Julius Caesar did not finally conquer Gaul until 58 B.C., and it took almost another century before Britain was incorporated into the Roman Empire.

The oldest surviving records of the Celts appear in *The Histories* by Herodotus, written 2,500 years ago. He mentions the Celts almost casually as living beyond the Pillars of Hercules, the Straits of Gibraltar. The casual reference indicates that the Greeks considered the Celts to be a major barbarian people. Ephorus, writing a century later, considered the Celts to be one of the four great barbarian peoples. The other three were the Scythians, Persians, and Libyans.[3]

Four hundred years after Herodotus, Julius Caesar wrote *The Gallic War*, which included his experiences with the Celts. Much of this knowledge was gained first-hand, but he must also have learned a great deal from his friend, Diviciacus, the Celtic leader who travelled with him on one campaign. Diviciacus stayed at Caesar's home in Rome when he gave an impressive speech to the Senate. This friendship even survived major problems caused by the treachery of Diviciacus' brother, Dumnorix.[4] Caesar's account was largely impartial, but naturally he used his writings as propaganda to gain support for his campaigns and consequently portrayed the Celts as barbarians.

Caesar wrote that in Gaul only two classes of people were of any importance: the druids and the knights. The rest were treated almost as slaves. The druids were the judges in disputes, priests in worship and sacrifices, and the teachers. The druids were exempt from paying taxes and from military service.[5]

Archaeologists have split the early history of the Celts into two parts: the Hallstatt and the La Tène. The Hallstatt period was from about 700 to 500 B.C. and was named after a site in Austria where many ancient Celtic artifacts have been found.

The Hallstatt Celts discovered iron, a much more valuable and versatile metal than that used by their Bronze Age ancestors.[6] Iron weapons and utensils were traded all over the Mediterranean, making the Celts wealthy and powerful. The Hallstatt Celts spoke Gaelic, which was to become one of the most important of Celtic languages.

About 500 B.C. the La Tène Celts emerged from Switzerland. They used two-wheeled war chariots to conquer most of Europe. It is possible that they were the inventors of spoked wheels. People were terrified of the La Tène Celts, but at the same time they were impressed with their advanced technology, skilled craftsmanship, and religious fervor. The La Tène Celts were ruled by wealthy, powerful chieftains who were in a position to encourage and patronize the arts. As a result, Celtic art blossomed. The Celtic craftsmen made swords and shields with intricate designs. Beautiful jewelry was made from gold and bronze. Pottery and stonework were beautifully decorated. Fortunately, much of this creativity has survived.

Herodotus, the Greek historian, was the first to record the name "Celt" in the fifth century B.C. By this stage they were a powerful group of numerous tribes who called themselves *Keltoi*. These tribes shared a powerful priesthood, similar religious traditions, and a common political organization. They were well organized, highly creative, and striking in appearance.[6]

Contemporary writings and archaeological research show that the ancient Celts were not simply primitive barbarians. They had a complex legal system. Their medical knowledge was highly advanced. In 1935, a skull was found with two large holes cut on either side of the brain. The later healing of the bone showed that Celtic surgeons had successfully performed brain surgery twice on the same patient. Many other such skulls have been found, showing that brain surgery was not uncommon.[7] Under Celtic law the tribe had the responsibility for caring for the sick, and treatment and hospital care were available for anyone who needed it.

Celtic culture has lasted in many parts of the world, particularly in Wales and Ireland. The Romans never conquered Ireland, and Celtic traditions prospered there, as well as in Wales,

Scotland, and Cornwall. In the fifth and sixth centuries A.D. many people from Cornwall and Wales returned to mainland Europe to escape the Saxons, taking the Celtic traditions with them.

A Celtic revival in the eighteenth century introduced the Celtic teachings to a wide new audience, and this interest has continued to grow to the present day. There is more interest in Celtic traditions, Celtic languages, Celtic art, and Celtic music today than at any other time in history.

The ancient Celts liked surrounding themselves with beautiful objects. Their weapons were intricately carved and decorated with beautiful, precious stones. They decorated their feasting halls with silks and linens containing beautiful designs. Their clothing was woven with gold thread. Their gorgeous neck adornments, rings, helmets, and other decorations can be found in most large museums around the world, a testimony to their skill. They were influenced by the classical designs of the Greeks, but adapted them and made them distinctly their own. The Celtic love of feasting had a direct relationship to their art, and a popular saying was, "Celtic art owed much to Celtic thirst."[8]

Their homes were comfortable, but not overly luxurious. In Britain their houses were round, with a central fireplace. A hole was cut in the roof that allowed smoke to escape but did not allow rain in.[9] In Europe their homes were often oval or square. The homes of the knights, druids, and other wealthy people were very large, with beautiful hangings on the walls.[10]

Daily life varied depending on the region and the climate. They made bread in ovens and used cooking pits in the ground in which entire animals could be roasted. When they could get it they enjoyed wine, but milk, beer, and mead were plentiful. Pork, either fresh or salted, and fish were the favorite meals at feasts. They made cheese, kept bees, and grew herbs, both for food and medication. Sheep provided mutton and also wool, which was woven and made into clothes. The variety of sheep they bred did not need to be shorn, as the wool could be plucked from them.[11]

Individual Celts could not own land. The land was owned by the whole tribe and divided into a number of areas. A large area was common ground that everyone could use for pastoral and agricultural purposes. Other areas were reserved for the tribal leaders as recompense for the work they did for the tribe as a whole. Individuals who had their own plots paid taxes on it, so the entire tribe could benefit. They also made up the army in times of war and had the right to vote.

Celtic farmers were very advanced. In the first century B.C. Pliny the Elder recorded that the Celtic plow was better than the Roman one. He also mentioned that the Celts manured their fields and had a type of harvesting machine that was pulled by an ox and plucked ears of corn.[12]

Feasting was an extremely popular pastime. The Celts drank an ale called *cuirm* which was usually made from barley, though rye, oats, and wheat could also be used when necessary. Most people made their own ale, but professionally brewed ale was also available.[13] Many contemporary writers commented on the vast amounts of liquor drunk at their feasts. According to Posidonius who wrote in the first century B.C., the nobles drank wine imported from Italy and the south of France and the poorer people drank a wheaten beer.

The Celts enjoyed hunting, physical sports, feasting, playing board games, and listening to the stories and poetry of the bards. They were articulate people who enjoyed expressing themselves. They were also highly religious and paid strict observance to the teachings of the druids. They were quickly aroused, but equally quick to forgive. They were warlike yet chivalrous.

The favorite board game was *fidchell*, which means "wooden wisdom." This game is similar to chess, with two teams lined up on opposite sides of a wooden board. This game is mentioned frequently in Celtic mythology, showing how popular it was.[14]

The Celts were a tall, fair race, with attractive features. The women, in particular, were considered extremely beautiful by the Romans, who also considered them more dangerous than the men. The Celtic women were extremely brave and did not hesitate to fight alongside the men. Celtic women certainly enjoyed more power and prestige than women in most other cultures of the time. For instance, they were able to inherit property and rise to positions of leadership. The Romans found this equality astonishing.

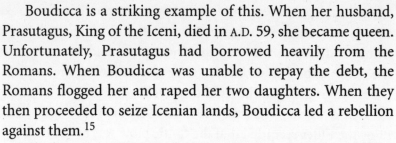

Boudicca is a striking example of this. When her husband, Prasutagus, King of the Iceni, died in A.D. 59, she became queen. Unfortunately, Prasutagus had borrowed heavily from the Romans. When Boudicca was unable to repay the debt, the Romans flogged her and raped her two daughters. When they then proceeded to seize Icenian lands, Boudicca led a rebellion against them.[15]

The Roman conquest of Gaul marked the beginning of the end for the Celts as a separate group. The invading armies became better organized, the spread of Christianity had a marked effect, and the Celts gradually declined in power and became assimilated into the other peoples of Europe.

However, they never entirely disappeared. It is estimated that today some two and a half million people speak a Celtic language. This is a high percentage of the sixteen million people who live in Celtic countries. Irish is the first official language of Eire and about a third of the population is able to speak it. The Irish government supports the use of the language by subsidizing Irish-speaking radio stations, newspapers, and magazines. Irish buses show the destination in Irish. "An Lar," for instance, means "City Center." Irish is also an official language of the European Economic Community.

CHAPTER TWO

The Druids

If you asked a hundred people who they thought the druids were, you would be likely to get a hundred different answers. Words such as "Stonehenge," "mistletoe," and "oak trees" would crop up again and again, but few people would know much about these important figures from our past.

Today many people in the West look towards the East for truth and enlightenment, somehow overlooking the highly evolved and developed Western mystery tradition. Perhaps the lure of something foreign and exotic is more appealing than a "home-grown" spiritual system. Like many others I have been captivated and entranced by the mystic East, so I can understand these feelings. It is a good thing to look at other traditions, but we should also examine our own spiritual heritage before embracing others.

The druids play a pivotal part in the Western mystery tradition. Unfortunately, they chose not to record their teachings and taught by a process of rote learning. Ordinary correspondence was done in Greek, but the druids did not allow their teachings to be written down. There were two reasons for this. First, as Julius Caesar recorded, they "did not wish the rule to become common property," and second, they did not want

their students to neglect memory. Julius Caesar wrote: "They commit to memory immense amounts of poetry. And some continue twenty years in their education; neither is it held lawful to commit these things (the druidic teachings) to writing, though in almost all public transactions and private accounts they use the Greek characters." In fact, surviving Celtic inscriptions and texts date back just as far as Roman ones.

The Celts came from Europe to Britain between three and four thousand years ago. They were skilled craftspeople who already knew how to make bronze weapons. They travelled widely, had cultural interests, and were highly creative. As they initially did not have a written language, a great deal of what they had to say was recorded in magnificent decorative work, much of which has survived to the present day. They were particularly fascinated with glass, and this is recorded, not only in surviving glasswork, but also in many of their stories. Early in his career King Arthur fought a battle in a glass castle, and when he died he was transported to the Otherworld in a glass boat. At one time Glastonbury was known as the Glass Island.

The Celts traded all over the known world: gold was brought in from the Orient, glass beads came from Egypt, amber from Scandinavia, and wine and oil from Italy. Iron swords, more than two thousand years old, have been found with hilts and sheaths beautifully decorated with gold, ivory, and amber.

They left their mark all over the British Isles. Stonehenge was built on the Salisbury Plains some three to four thousand years ago, an astonishing feat of engineering.[1] The outer circle consisted of fifty-six sarsen stones, some weighing thirty tons. Inside this was a circle of sixty blue stones transported from the Prescelly Mountains of Wales. Inside this was a horseshoe of stones, divided into pairs with lintels joining them at the top. Finally, there was another horseshoe of blue stones, again with lintels. We can only guess why it was built, as the druids usually chose to worship in sacred groves and sanctuaries. However, it is believed that the gatherings of bards were held inside circles of stones. Stonehenge was probably a temple of the sun, as the vast circle of stones accurately marks midsummer, midwinter, and eclipses of the sun and moon. Stonehenge is the largest and most impressive of the almost three hundred stone circles erected in the British Isles.

It is likely that these stone circles were erected before the Celts arrived in Britain. Other forms of ancient religion were well established in Britain before the druids arrived. In fact, the Gaulish druids used to send their students to Britain to learn, which indicates a much older tradition than their own. Even if the Celts did not build these stone circles, the druids made good use of them.

The druids were so much in awe of the sun that they tried never to turn their backs to it. This tradition still survives today with the requirement of not turning one's back to royalty. Sun worship was widespread, with a number of sun gods, such as Lugh and Mac Gréine (son of the sun). He was married to Eire, who gave her name to Ireland. Bel, "the shining one," was the god who gave his name to Beltaine.

The Celts left their mark on the landscape in other ways. No one who has seen the graceful lines of the Uffington White Horse is ever likely to forget it. It is a 360-foot-long horse, carved out of the green hillside above the Vale of Uffington in Berkshire, to reveal the white chalk beneath. This racing horse is constructed from just seven graceful lines. Its particular beauty comes from its simplicity, and it represents one of the first of many such horses. Horses, of course, were extremely important to the Celts, representing energy, power, and fruitfulness. One of the Celtic goddesses, Epona, was a horse goddess, so it is not surprising to see horses venerated in this way. Epona was even worshiped by the Romano-British cavalry and was the only Celtic goddess to be officially honored in Rome. The Uffington horse dates from between the first century B.C. and the first century A.D. It was carved originally by local Celts to signify their territory, and possibly to venerate Epona. Horses were also depicted on Celtic coins and numerous artifacts.[2]

It is interesting to note that even today people stand in the eye of the Uffington horse, then close their eyes, turn around three times, and make a wish. This ancient tradition indicates the special magical properties the Uffington White Horse is believed to have.[3]

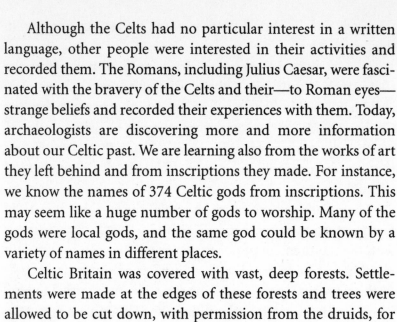

Although the Celts had no particular interest in a written language, other people were interested in their activities and recorded them. The Romans, including Julius Caesar, were fascinated with the bravery of the Celts and their—to Roman eyes—strange beliefs and recorded their experiences with them. Today, archaeologists are discovering more and more information about our Celtic past. We are learning also from the works of art they left behind and from inscriptions they made. For instance, we know the names of 374 Celtic gods from inscriptions. This may seem like a huge number of gods to worship. Many of the gods were local gods, and the same god could be known by a variety of names in different places.

Celtic Britain was covered with vast, deep forests. Settlements were made at the edges of these forests and trees were allowed to be cut down, with permission from the druids, for cultivation purposes. There were heavy penalties for cutting down a tree without permission. Firewood was obtained from dead trees and branches that had fallen to the ground, so there was no need to cut trees for this purpose. The expression "touch wood" or "knock on wood" dates back to this veneration of trees and shows the emotive power that wood still has today.[4]

The mystery schools were held in the middle of these forests. From Samhaine to Beltaine (the dark half of the year) the students would study at these schools. The daily routine was arduous: twelve hours a day, seven days a week. The material covered would include religious lore, ogham, history of sacred sites and individuals, astronomy, astrology, mathematics, and music, as well as poetry. Huge amounts of material had to be memorized, including the genealogies of kings, laws, customs, stories, and poems. In the bardic schools, the students would be given a topic late every afternoon. At midnight the students would return to recite a poem they had written on the given topic. This would then be evaluated and commented upon by their teachers. The remaining six months of the year would be spent with an experienced poet in the home of a chieftain learning how to compose verse in the real world.

After eight years of this intensive training, the student would qualify as a bard[5] and could then make a lucrative living composing for the families of chieftains or becoming a story-teller. Students could also, if considered suitable, carry on with their education for a further twelve years and become druids.

Bards could make extremely good livings, because they could not refuse any gift offered to them. Taliesen received a hundred racehorses, a hundred purple cloaks, a hundred bracelets, fifty brooches, and a fine sword from one of his patrons. It has been recorded that some bards took advantage of this tradition by asking for outrageous gifts. Bards were feared, also, because they could create songs designed to ridicule and humiliate their enemies. The bards must have made an impressive sight, striding into a hall carrying a golden branch with several bells tied to it. The branch indicated authority and the sound of the bells told the audience to be quiet. William Blake puts the feelings and expectations of the audience wonderfully well in his *Songs of Experience*:

> O Hear the voice of the bard
> Who present, past and future sees
> Whose ears have heard the holy Word
> That walked among the ancient trees...[6]

The Celts divided their intellectual elite into three groups: druids, bards, and ovates. The bards were the poets, and the druids and ovates were religious and political officials. The druids were considered senior to the ovates. The druids were more involved in theology and philosophy than the ovates, who specialized in divination and sacrifices. However, there was a considerable overlap in the duties, and a druid could officiate at a sacrifice and an ovate become involved in philosophical discussions. Although the ovates usually carried out the sacrifices, a druid had to be present.

The ovates used augury, divination, and prophecy. Auguries were based on signs and omens, such as the flight paths of birds and observation of animals. Boudicca released a hare before a battle and watched its path to predict her own success. The shapes of clouds and images found in the flames of fires were interpreted. A form of crystal gazing was done by gazing into

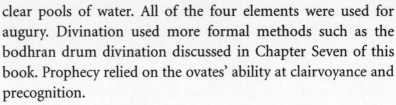

clear pools of water. All of the four elements were used for augury. Divination used more formal methods such as the bodhran drum divination discussed in Chapter Seven of this book. Prophecy relied on the ovates' ability at clairvoyance and precognition.

The druids wielded enormous power over the society they lived in. Diodorus of Sicily wrote in the first century B.C. that, "Those men called by us philosophers and theologians are held in great honor by them; they call them druids…and no sacrifice may be performed without a druid present…for only they speak the language of the gods." This gives us another insight into why the druids kept their teachings so secret. Knowledge was power, and only they knew "the language of the gods."

Unfortunately, over the last two thousand years, a great deal of misinformation has been spread about the druids. People at different times have cast the druids in different roles: as noble savages; as romantic, caring philanthropists; as lustful warriors; and so on. You can find druids portrayed in all of these roles, and many more, in the literature of the last three hundred years. Because so little is known about them, people have been able to make of the druids whatever they wished.

We do not know where the druids came from originally or how their philosophy developed. Many people claim that they brought their knowledge and wisdom from Atlantis.[7] Others say it came from the East as part of the Indo-European tradition. Certainly, there are a number of similarities in the beliefs of the druids and the Brahmins. Both believed in reincarnation, both carried consecrated staffs, both revered white horses and circles, and both usually worshiped outdoors.

However, even though some of their wisdom may have come originally from the East, the knowledge went both ways. Clement of Alexandria wrote that Pythagoras went to study with the druids in Gaul. He called druidism "a religion of philosophers." Hecateus of Abdera who had travelled widely, held the druids in high esteem. He also recorded that Pythagoras was taught by a druid called Abaris.

Julius Caesar recorded that both the druids and noblemen in Gaul were held in honor. The druids served as legal officials, resolving conflicts and deciding on suitable penalties. Anyone who disobeyed the druidic verdict was barred from sacrifice. This was the severest of all punishments as it meant the person was termed wicked and godless.

The archdruid remained so until his death, when another was appointed. At times, the druids had to vote on a suitable successor and this sometimes led to violence.

Caesar also recorded that the druids met once a year at a site considered to be in the very center of Gaul. At this time all outstanding disputes were resolved. It is thought that this annual meeting was held on the site of the present-day Chartres Cathedral. The Irish had a similar druidic shrine at Tara, and the Isle of Anglesey served the same purpose for the British druids.

The Romans regarded the druids as a major threat. The druids living on the sacred Isle of Anglesey constantly incited the Welsh people to rebel against the Roman invaders. Finally, in A.D. 59, the governor, Suetonius Paulinus, attempted to wipe the druids out before carrying on to punish the Welsh. He did this in a well-organized campaign. The cavalry crossed on their horses, swimming alongside them when the water became too deep. The infantry followed on flat-bottomed barges. They were greeted by rows of druidesses, dressed in black, brandishing burning torches and screaming defiance at the Romans. The soldiers hesitated until Suetonius Paulinus broke the spell with shouted remarks about soldiers who were scared of a group of fanatical women.[8] The first defenses were beaten easily and the battle carried on inland, where the druids tried to protect their sacred groves. The soldiers killed the priests and were about to destroy the forests when Paulinus heard the astonishing news that Boudicca's army had destroyed Colchester and was heading towards London.

The arrival of Christianity was another threat to the druids. The Romans, in particular, regarded druidism as a pagan religion and tried to stamp it out. Although no idols have been found among druid remains, Julius Caesar declared that "the countries of druids were full of idols." All the same, there appear to be early links between druidism and Christianity. Certainly, the Celts were among the first to accept Christianity, even before Rome.[9]

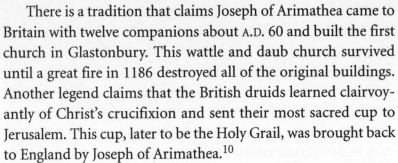

There is a tradition that claims Joseph of Arimathea came to Britain with twelve companions about A.D. 60 and built the first church in Glastonbury. This wattle and daub church survived until a great fire in 1186 destroyed all of the original buildings. Another legend claims that the British druids learned clairvoyantly of Christ's crucifixion and sent their most sacred cup to Jerusalem. This cup, later to be the Holy Grail, was brought back to England by Joseph of Arimathea.[10]

In fact, many of the teachings of the druids were very similar to those of Christianity, and consequently it was not difficult for many people to accept the teachings of the new religion along with their earlier beliefs. It is believed that Bran the Blessed, an archdruid, was an early convert to Christianity. He was sent to Rome as a hostage and returned to Wales in his old age to preach the gospel. Many druids embraced Christianity, because they could see that all religions have the same ultimate basis, and it was relatively easy to encompass Christian rites and beliefs in the druid philosophy. The early Church was anxious for this to happen and Pope Gregory I (540–604) issued a bull allowing the druid and Christian beliefs to intermingle and become one.

The druids were able to teach as many as 60,000 students at a time in thirty-one different schools.[11] Mnemonics were used extensively. The ogham letters, as we shall see later, were of great importance as memory aids.

The training of the novitiates could last twenty years. Only freemen were allowed to attend these schools. At the initiation ceremonies the novitiates wore a robe of three colors: white, blue, and green. These colors stood for light, truth, and hope. The students were tonsured to free the important center at the top of the head.[11] This tradition still exists, of course, in the Christian Church with the tonsure of monks. The druidic tonsure was from ear to ear, rather than the circular tonsure later used by the Christian Church. Druids also wore beards, and these were not trimmed, being encouraged to grow as long as possible. Laymen were allowed to grow mustaches, but not beards.[11]

Once the long period of training was over, the druids became priests, bards, or ovates. The priests wore white robes, the bards blue, and the ovates green. The bards were primarily concerned with literature, and the ovates were the experts at divination. However, there was some overlap between the divisions.

The Celts regarded themselves as being especially chosen by God. The very name "Celt" comes from *kelu,* which means "children of the most high God." Nature was venerated. Earth was believed to be the mother of all mankind. Trees, which grow from the earth, were especially precious, symbolizing the earthmother's protection. This is why the druids worshiped in sacred groves of trees. The holy Isle of Anglesey was venerated because of the many groves of oak trees found there.

The druids believed in the transmigration of souls and at one time thought that clouds were made from the souls of people waiting to be reincarnated.[12] As they had not yet reached perfection, they were not ready to unite with the sun. Souls who no longer needed earthly reincarnation were believed to live on the moon until it was time for them to evolve further. The sun was believed to be composed of pure souls, living in a state of complete bliss, but even this was not the ultimate. After being purified three times in the sun, the soul was able to progress even further and reach Paradise. Meteors transported the souls of druids directly to Paradise. The druids believed so strongly in reincarnation that some Roman writers recorded instances of money being lent that had to be repaid in the next lifetime. The druid theory of reincarnation was that they would come back again as one of their own descendants, just as they in turn were the reincarnation of an ancestor. As the soul became more and more evolved, longer periods would pass between earthly incarnations. Unlike many religions that believe in reincarnation, the druids regarded being reincarnated again into this world as a good thing, and the soul eventually ceased its earthly existence reluctantly.

The Romans almost succeeded in wiping out the druids. In fact, the term "druid" almost disappeared.[13] However, the druidic teachings continued in a quiet way over the following centuries, simply adding to the mystery.

In tenth century Wales, the bards were assessed and placed into different grades.[14] After this, the order gradually declined

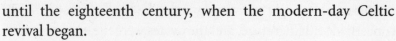

until the eighteenth century, when the modern-day Celtic revival began.

At this time a Glamorgan stonemason, Edward Williams, declared that he and a friend were the last two remaining Welsh bards. He called himself Iolo Morganwag, and set about recreating his vision of what the druids were really like. Unfortunately, he caused a great deal of damage with his invented theories, but his enthusiasm also led to the reinstatement of the famous Welsh Eisteddfods.[15] Around this time various groups began, such as the Ancient Order of Druids, and many still exist today. Arguably the leading group in Britain today is the Order of Bards, Ovates, and Druids.[16] There are also groups in France, the United States, Australasia, and other countries. Many people prefer to remain independent and call themselves druids even though they do not belong to any organized groups.[17]

Triads

Many of the teachings of the druids are grouped into triads, partly as an aid to memory, but also to summarize and preserve their truths.[18] The concept of three is universal among the Indo-European cultures, but the Celts took it further than anyone else. Indo-European society was itself a three-tiered structure. There was the priest to represent magico-religious activities, the warrior to represent the power of the sword, and the farmer to represent fertility and prosperity.

Unfortunately, only parts of the oldest triads survive. The tradition of triads survived the spread of Christianity and we can be grateful to the monks of the Middle Ages who recorded them, even though many were deliberately given a Christian slant. Diogenes Laertius mentioned in the second or third century B.C. that the druids taught by using triads.[19]

King Arthur had the honor of appearing in more triads than anyone else, though not all of the references to him are complimentary. Also, several triads were expanded into tetrads because of him. An example is the triad called "Three Exalted Prisoners," which has had the following sentence added: "And there was another prisoner who was even more famous, and this was Arthur."

The first native Celt to become a major influence in the Christian Church was Hilary, who became Bishop of Poitiers about 350. He wrote *De Trinitate*, which outlined the concept of the Holy Trinity. Consequently, it is possible that the Trinity owes more to Celtic theology than to the Judaic tradition.

A large number of triads have been preserved. Unfortunately, not all of them make a great deal of sense today, because the information they were written down to preserve was never otherwise recorded. Here are some examples of triads:

Three things are found everywhere:
God, Truth, and the Circle of Knowledge, and to know them is to become part of them.

Three things that can never be known: the plane of existence of God, the length of Eternity, and the love of God.

The three characteristics of God are: complete life, complete knowledge, and complete power.

The three Unities are: one God, one truth, and one point of liberty.

The three greatest tumults of the world: the Deluge, the Crucifixion, and the Day of Judgment.

Three candles that lighten darkness: truth, nature, and knowledge.

Three qualities of a good man: Truth in the heart, strength in the arm, and honesty in the tongue.

Three things that are always ready in a good man's house: beer, a bath, and a good fire.

Three things that constitute a good doctor: a complete cure, leaving no blemish behind, and a painless examination.

Three keys that unlock thoughts: drunkenness, trustfulness, and love.

The three doors by which falsehood enters: anger in outlining the case, doubtful information, and evidence from a bad memory.

Diogenes Laertius noted that the religious system of the druids was based on three precepts: to worship the Gods, to do no evil, and to act with courage.

Three was a sacred number to the Celts. It linked myths, legends, and deities together. Many of their sculptures show figures with three faces. The Celtic religion was dominated by three gods: Taranis, the thunder god; Esus; and Teutates. The leaders of Celtic society were also three: druids, bards, and ovates. The number three comes up time and again in everything associated with the Celts, from literature to craftwork.

The Other Worlds

The druids believed that, in addition to the world we live in, there were two other worlds coexisting at the same time. These are the Otherworld and the Underworld.

The Otherworld (or Otherworlds) is symbolized as being higher or above this world. It was possible to enter it through hidden, secret doorways that could open anywhere. These doorways usually appeared at ancient burial grounds or sacred groves. Celtic legends often recount stories of people crossing the veil and entering the Otherworld. It was easier to cross over into another world when the Earth was in a state of flux. Consequently, dawn, dusk, and full moon were excellent times, as were fog, storms, lightning, and eclipses. Fog, in particular, was regarded as creating an open door between the worlds. People could easily walk into other worlds at this time, and beings from other worlds could just as easily cross over into ours as well. These beings could be anything from ancestors to elementals. Fog was called the "cloak of the gods."

The Other Worlds

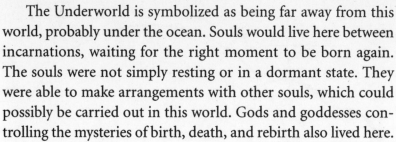

The Underworld is symbolized as being far away from this world, probably under the ocean. Souls would live here between incarnations, waiting for the right moment to be born again. The souls were not simply resting or in a dormant state. They were able to make arrangements with other souls, which could possibly be carried out in this world. Gods and goddesses controlling the mysteries of birth, death, and rebirth also lived here.

The Earth world, between the other two worlds, was inhabited by animals, humans, and the gods and goddesses relating to nature. In many ways, the Earth world contained much from the other two worlds, because it overlapped them. The upper zone contained the weather, spirit flight, clouds, and augury obtained from the flight patterns of birds. The middle zone contained plants, animals, and humans and was divided into North, South, East, and West. The lower zone was inhabited by fairies, gods, and goddesses. It was related to wells, sacred springs, lakes, caves, and burial mounds. It is a negative zone, relating to the darker, hidden forces.

The Otherworld, Underworld, and earthly world were divided into fifths: north, south, east, west, and center. The center overlapped the other sections and was home to the places where it was possible to move from one world to another.

Death, of course, also took a soul from the Earth to the Otherworld, and a death in the Otherworld took a soul to Earth. In other words, death simply meant that a soul moved from one world to another.

Circles

The druids had three Circles of Existence showing the basis of creation. It is possible that these are represented in ancient rock monuments, such as Avebury. These circles are known as Abred, Gwynedd, and Ceugant.[20] In the beginning there was nothing but God and Annwn (pronounced *Annoon*). It was essential for bards to be able to remember their prenatal life and birth, and this was known as "the memory of Annwn."[21]

The innermost circle is Abred, the place where the inner and outer worlds meet. Everything begins here and returns again at its death. This is the home of Annwn, the spirit world. Abred is the realm of Matter.

The middle circle, Gwynedd, is the realm of Blessedness and Purity. Life here is good and pure, having triumphed over evil.

The outer circle, Ceugant, is the realm of Infinities. It spreads out into infinity, but ultimately circles back into Abred. Ceugant is often represented, not by a simple circle, but by a series of divergent rays. This is the home of God.

The druids usually taught by a process of question and answer. Here is a quote from the *Bardass,* a two-volume book of Celtic wisdom compiled by Llewellyn Sion of Glamorgan in the sixteenth century:

Q. Whence didst thou proceed?

A. I came from the Great World, having my beginning in Annwn.

Q. Where art thou now? and how camest thou to what thou art?

A. I am in the Little World, whither I came having traversed the circle of Abred, and now I am a Man, at its termination and extreme limits.

Q. What wert thou before thou didst become a man, in the circle of Abred?

A. I was in Annwn the least possible that was capable of life and the nearest possible to absolute death; and I came in every form and through every form capable of a body and life to the state of man along the circle of Abred, where my condition was severe and grievous during the age of ages, ever since I was parted in Annwn from the dead, by the gift of God, and His great generosity, and His unlimited and endless love.

Q. Through how many different forms didst thou come, and what happened unto thee?

A. Through every form capable of life, in water, in earth, in air. And there happened unto me every severity, every hardship, every evil, and every suffering, and but little was the goodness or Gwynned before I became a man…And there can be no full and perfect love that does not produce those things which are necessary to lead to the knowledge that causes Gwynned.[22]

Mistletoe

The druids regarded mistletoe as being the essence of life. It was known as *Druad-lus,* the "Druid's Plant." Twigs from the mistletoe were given at the time of New Year to confer the gods' blessing on the household. These relate very much to fertility and were intended to give the recipient a fruitful year, in children, cattle, and crops.[23] The pleasant tradition of kissing under the mistletoe comes originally from ancient beliefs relating to this fertility and sexuality.

Pliny recorded that "Nothing is more sacred to the druids than the mistletoe and the tree on which it grows, especially if it be an oak. They seek the oak tree for their sacred groves, and no ceremony is complete without its branches. Whatever grows on the tree is sent from heaven, a sign that the tree has been chosen by the god."[24]

Mistletoe is a rare plant that grows as a parasite on apple, lime, and hawthorn trees, and occasionally on oaks. It was especially sacred when found on an oak tree. The oak was a symbol of the sun to the Celts, and the berries of the mistletoe represented the moon. In fact, they look like small moons. Consequently, mistletoe on an oak tree indicated fertility, as it meant the earth goddess was growing on the tree of the sun god. Because this occurred so seldom, it is possible that the druids grafted mistletoe onto certain oak trees. It was cut with great ceremony by an initiate dressed in white robes and with bare feet that had been ritually washed in pure water. A gold knife was used for the cutting, and this represented the young sickle moon. (However, some authorities claim the gold knife symbolized the sun.)

At *Alban Arthuan,* the winter solstice, the druids would accept a small offering in exchange for a small spray of consecrated mistletoe to ensure that the coming year would be a happy one. These sprigs of mistletoe were worn around the neck and later hung over doorways to protect the home. Modern-day druids still carry sprigs of holly and mistletoe at their ceremonies.

Mistletoe was also revered in Scandinavia where the tradition of kissing under the mistletoe began. Enemies would meet under the mistletoe, if they wished to be reconciled, and exchange a kiss of peace.

Mistletoe was also used as a medicine, as indicated by its old name of *All-Heal.* It was said that it would immediately stop an epileptic fit. It was also used as a nerve tonic and to heighten psychic awareness.

Trees

The idea of a world tree is common to many groups of people, and trees have been worshiped all around the world. It was often known as the Tree of Knowledge or the Tree of Life. Symbolically, the tree stands for eternal life and reflects the tree of life inside all of us.

Different races have visualized this tree in many forms. Most Western civilizations believed it had its roots in hell and its branches in heaven, but some cultures had it the other way around. The Hebrews, for instance, have a tree of life that "spreads downward from above and is entirely bathed in the sun." The Micronesians have a legend which says the world began with a giant upside-down tree which had its roots in the sky and its branches touching the oceans. In these branches was a woman who formed the earth by sprinkling sand on the sea. The Brahmins had their Asvatta tree to symbolize creation. It also had its roots in the heavens, with the branches in the world. Its leaves were said to be sacred songs, while its buds were the pleasures of the senses.

Different faiths tried to outdo each other with the size of their tree of life. The Muslims had the Tooba which casts its shade over all of paradise. It was said that a man on horseback would take more than one hundred years to ride around it.

Indisputably, the most famous of these symbolic trees is the Scandinavian Yggdrasil, the tree of Odin. This tree had three roots which reached down into the three realms of the gods. The leaves were the clouds and its fruits were the stars. The first man, Ash, was said to have arisen from this tree. There have been claims that Yggdrasil was an Ash tree, which makes the Scandinavian ideas similar to the Greeks, who also believed that man sprang from a cosmogenic Ash.

Tree worship was very common in India. It was said that Gautama, the Buddha, spent forty-three incarnations as a tree spirit. He used to receive spiritual insights during his meditations under the Bodhi tree.[25]

The Celts believed the tree of life was inside all of us. The human backbone was the seat of life. God was believed to have made the spine from willow wood, as it was so flexible and pliable. As the person ages the back gradually bends like an old tree.

Dreams

The druids were exceptionally good at divination with dreams, and many of their rites involved creating the right situation for dreams to occur. They did not interpret them in the way we commonly do today. They thought that as soon as you tried to analyze a dream the prophetic element disappeared.

Upon waking, the Celts would lie in a meditative state and consciously try to relive the dream. Any thoughts were allowed to enter their minds as they daydreamed about their dreams. Then they would consciously become each part of the dream. If the dream involved an oak tree and a dragon, for instance, they would become the oak tree and experience the tree's feelings through the dream, before doing the same thing with the dragon.

Finally, they would talk to the various parts of the dream. In the above example, a druid might ask the tree, "I know that you are important to my dream, but I can't understand why. Why are you in my dream?" He would wait for a reply to come into his mind and then ask other questions.

The Poems of Amairgen

Amairgen was one of the first druids in Ireland. He was also a warrior and poet. Three of his poems have been preserved, the most famous of which is a powerful incantation which he chanted when he first set foot on Ireland. This lay is still used by druids today, and you will find it helpful to recite it before undertaking any of the divination procedures described in this book. There have been many translations of "The Song of Amairgen," but my favorite is the version by the nineteenth-century Celtic scholar, M. d'Arbois de Jubainville:

I am the Wind that blows over the sea;
I am a Wave of the Ocean;
I am the Murmur of the billows;
I am the Ox of the Seven Combats;
I am the Vulture on the rock;
I am a Ray of the Sun;
I am the fairest of Plants;
I am a Wild Boar in valour;
I am a Salmon in the Water;
I am a Lake in the plain;
I am the Craft of the artificer;
I am a Word of Science;
I am the Spear-point that gives battle;
I am the God that creates in the head of man the fire of
    thought.
Who is it that enlightens the assembly upon the mountain, if
    not I?
Who telleth the ages of the moon, if not I?
Who showeth the place where the sun goes to rest, if not I?

This poem,[26] and a similar one by Taliesen, appear to indicate that the Celts believed in reincarnation in a number of forms. Transformation into a wide variety of different forms is also depicted in "The Cattle-Raid of Cooley," an ancient Irish epic. In this story, two swineherds go through a series of metamorphoses, becoming bulls, ravens, stags, warriors, water monsters, demons, and even aquatic worms.

CHAPTER THREE

The Eightfold Year

The Celts had a thirteen-month year, twelve months that correspond roughly to our own and a three-day month at the end of October, leading up to Samhaine.

The year was divided into two halves, light and dark, warm and cold. Samhaine marked the start of the dark half of the year. Marriage was not allowed in the dark half of the year. Beltaine was the start of the light half of the year, and was the second most important festival after Samhaine.[1] Between Samhaine and Beltaine were Imbolc and Lughnasadh, creating four quarters. These four were all Fire Festivals that were celebrated over a period of three days, before, during, and after the event.

The Fire Festivals were in turn divided by the solstices and equinoxes, creating the eightfold year. The fire festivals were solar festivals, and the remaining four were lunar, creating an equal number of male and female festivals.

Each of these eight times was especially good for divination as the veils temporarily lifted and gave easier access to the other worlds. Divining can be done throughout the year, but more powerful insights can be gained at these times.

In 1897, a huge bronze calendar was found at Coligny, close to Lyon. This calendar, dating from the first century A.D., proves that the Celts were master mathematicians. They could calculate important dates in the Celtic year with this calendar. The calendar shows that during the month of Rivros, which means "great month of the feast," a huge festival was held in Gaul. This is exactly the same time of year as the Irish Lughnasadh. The Coligny Calendar was originally about five feet long and three feet high. Only about half of this engraved bronze calendar has been found, but it is sufficient to show how skillful the Celts were at astronomy, astrology, and mathematical calculation. This calendar is one of the oldest examples of writing in a Celtic language. Although Roman numbers and letters are used, the words are Celtic.[2] The calendar reckons periods of time by nights, rather than days.[3] Julius Caesar wrote, "They count periods of time not by the number of days but by the number of nights; and in reckoning birthdays and the new moon and the new years their unit of reckoning is the night followed by the day."[3]

Samhaine (November 1st)

Samhaine marks the first day of the Celtic New Year, which actually began at sunset on October 31st (Halloween). It was the most important festival of the year for the druids, marking the end of one pastoral year and the start of the next. It was regarded as belonging to neither the preceding year nor the following one, but to stand entirely on its own.[4] At this time laws were made, tribal elders met, and suitable people became warriors.[5]

People used to fear that the waning sun meant that the world was going to end. They were scared of the night, which they believed was the home of ghosts and spirits of the dead returning to their earthly home. For these reasons, they tried to prolong daylight by lighting huge bonfires and making sacrifices to the gods.

At Samhaine the gates to the Otherworlds opened and the inhabitants could cross over and avenge misdeeds that had been done to them. All sorts of evil was reputed to happen at this time. Halloween represents the survival of this belief. The ancients regarded the entire day of November 1st as a time when people could come across from the other worlds, so the entire day was a time of excitement, rather than just the evening.[5] All fires were extinguished at this time and had to be rekindled from a ceremonial fire lit by the druids.

The druids made their sacred drink, *La Mas Ushal*, at Samhaine, and drank it in honor of the god of fruitfulness.[6] It was made from apples, sugar, and ale and was drunk to ensure the germination of seeds under the ground in the dark time of the year.

The Christian Church took over this festival and renamed November 1st All Hallows' Day and November 2nd All Saints' Day.

Alban Arthuan (December 21st)

This is the Winter Solstice, marking the shortest day of the year. It marks the death of the old sun and the birth of the dark half of the year. Bede, the eighth-century Christian scholar, wrote that the winter solstice was called *Modranicht*, the Mother Night, and was the most important sacred occasion of the year.

Imbolc (February 1st)

This is a Fire Festival to celebrate the sun gaining strength again. Even though it is still winter, Imbolc commemorates the very first sign of spring and portends new beginnings. Farmers were able to celebrate the birth of the first spring lambs,[7] and the ewes started lactating.[8] Cakes were baked and offered to the gods in celebration. This festival was sacred to the fertility goddess, known as Brigit in Ireland and Brigantia in England. (The Christian Church renamed Brigit as Saint Bridget to allow people to celebrate this day without the pagan overtones).[9] In Ireland the first sod was traditionally tilled on this day. In Celtic tradition, a single candle was kept burning all day in every house. The Christians adopted this festival as Candlemas.

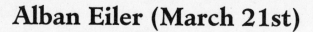

Alban Eiler (March 21st)

This is the Spring Equinox, the first day of spring. For the Celts it was a Bird Festival, and it was traditional to go bird-watching—and hunting—on this day. The Easter traditions of eggs and chicks derive from this festival.

Beltaine (May 1st)

Beltaine was named after Bel, the Celtic god who represented the sun. May Day was an annual fertility festival to welcome the start of summer and the light half of the year. The Celts celebrated it as a Flower Festival to welcome summer. They would dance around a living tree to celebrate its fruitfulness. The Maypole dates from this and relates back to primitive man's veneration of the phallus as the creator of life.[10] An ancient nursery rhyme commemorates this:

> Come lasses and lads, get leave of your dads,
> And away to the Maypole hie,
> For every he has got him a she,
> And the fiddler's standing by.
>
> —Anonymous

Huge bonfires were lit in praise of Bel for bringing victory over darkness. Two huge fires were also lit at the site of the festival to ward off evil and illness. Livestock were driven between these fires for purification, supervised by the druids.[11] Sir William Wilde quotes from an ancient manuscript in Trinity College Library: "*Beltine, i.e. Biltine, i.e.* lucky fire (bon-fire), *i.e.* two fires which used to be made by the lawgivers, or Druids, with great incantations, and they used to drive the cattle between them (to guard) against the diseases of each year. Or, Bel-dine: Bel was the name of an idol god. It was on it (*i.e.* that day) that the firstlings of every kind of cattle used to be exhibited as in the possession of Bel; *vide* Beldine."[12] The name Beltaine derives from this, as Bel-tinne means "the fires of Bel." T.G.E. Powell says the name Beltaine probably comes from Belenus, a god widely known in Northern Italy, Southeastern Gaul, and Noricum.[11] All household fires were put out and had to be relit from "the sacred fires of Bel," which were the rays of the sun, to represent a new start.[13] It was traditional for young couples to spend time in the woods on this day.

Alban Heruin (June 21st)

This is the summer solstice marking midsummer. The sun is at its highest now, and the oak tree is at its peak. Consequently, the druids celebrated an Oak Festival on this day.

Lughnasadh (August 1st)

This is the harvest festival to celebrate the marriage of Lugh[14] and Eire, Mother Earth. It marks the first day of autumn. The Celts celebrated it as a Grain Festival because Lugh was the Celtic Grain God. It was a festival to ensure the ripening of the crops rather than to give thanks for a good harvest.[15] It was a time for games, competitions, and weddings. Marriages made at this time could be annulled after one year, giving the couple a one-year trial marriage.[16] Early records state that this festival was celebrated for fifteen days. Christianity took this festival over, renaming it Lammas, to celebrate the first fruits.

Alban Elued (September 21st)

This is the autumn equinox, when day and night are equal in length. For the Celts it was the Festival of the Vine, a night of feasting and drinking. It marked the end of harvest-time.

Most of these festivals were adopted by the Christian Church. Because they played such an important part in the lives of the people, they could not be abolished. Samhaine became All Saints' Day and Imbolc became Candlemas. Lughnasadh became Lammas and continued the tradition of offering bread, only now it was offered at the local church rather than at a pagan shrine. As churches were often built on the sites of earlier pagan temples, the local people would not have noticed any major difference.

Because of its overtly sexual nature, the only festival the Christians could not absorb fully was Beltaine.

CHAPTER FOUR

Merlin

Merlin, Merlin, where art thou going
So early in the day with thy black dog?
I have come here to search for the way,
To find the red egg;
The red egg of the marine serpent,
By the seaside in the hollow of the stone.
I am going to seek in the valley
The green water cress and the golden grass
And the top branch of the oak,
In the wood by the side of the fountain.
Merlin, Merlin, retrace your steps;
Leave the branch on the oak
And the green water cress in the valley
As well as the golden grass;
And leave the red egg of the marine serpent
In the foam by the hollow of the stone.
Merlin! Merlin! Retrace thy steps
There is no diviner but God.

   —Translated by M. de Vollemarque from the Breton
      5th–6th century[1]

Merlin is unquestionably the most famous of all the druids. In fact, he may have been several people, rather than just one, because Merlin comes from *Myrrdin,* which means "wizard." One of the ancient Welsh triads states that Britain was called *Clas Myrrdin* (Merlin's Enclosure) before it was inhabited.

Geoffrey of Monmouth was just one of many writers who had the problem of explaining how Merlin appeared in different centuries. He may, of course, have been reincarnated as himself. It is more likely, though, that he is a composite of many druids who used the name Merlin.

There are historical records of two of them. Merlin ab Morvyn and Merlin Ambrosius appeared before Vortigern in A.D. 480. Ninety years later, Merlin Ambrosius was recorded as being at the court of Rydderch Hael.

Merlin Ambrosius was a friend of King Arthur's uncle, who was also called Ambrosius. Consequently, he is most likely the Merlin who guided the early career of King Arthur. "Ambrosius" means "immortal," which may explain how historical records can show him at two different places ninety years apart.

Merlin ab Morvyn was a druid, bard, and warrior who lived in the north of Britain. A legend about him claims that he went insane during a battle and retired to a forest in Scotland. The bulk of *The Black Book of Caermarthen* is attributed to him.[2] Geoffrey of Monmouth states that Merlin was born in Caermarthen, and in fact the name means "Myrddin's Town."

Geoffrey of Monmouth tells the story of how Merlin first came into prominence.[3] Apparently, King Vortigern started building a new fortress in Wales. His masons worked hard each day, but every night the foundations sank back into the earth. Vortigern was worried about the threat of a Saxon invasion and wanted the fortress to be completed as quickly as possible. He asked his seers for advice. They told him that the only way he could make the foundations secure was to sprinkle them with blood from a youth who had no human father. Vortigern's men searched the countryside in search of a boy with the right qualifications. As Merlin was believed to have been fathered by a demon, he was found and brought to the king. He managed to save his life by telling the king that he had had a vision of two dragons fighting each other in a subterranean lake below where the fortress was being built. Their battles were causing the foundations to slip into the ground.

Vortigern was skeptical, but ordered the ground to be dug up. Two dragons were found in their lairs, one white and the other red. Merlin proclaimed that the white dragon, symbolizing the Saxons, would win at first, but eventually would be beaten. As a result of this successful prophecy, the red dragon became the symbol of Wales. The Welsh Celts also accepted the dragon as their emblem. The background story of the two dragons is recorded in the *Mabinogion.*[4]

After this success, Merlin made many other prophecies. Vortigern was so impressed that he asked Merlin about his own future. Merlin told him that he would be burned to death in his castle. This prediction came true.

Merlin later became adviser to King Ambrosius. When he was killed, Merlin carried on in the same position for Ambrosius' brother, Uther Pendragon, who later became father of King Arthur. It was Merlin who suggested to Uther that he establish the knights of the round table. He also told Uther that his rightful heir would be found in a test involving pulling a sword from a stone.

Merlin was responsible for training and teaching the young Arthur in the ways of the druids and later became his adviser as well.[5]

Merlin was an archetypal seeker of truth, which is why his name is still so well known. Countless generations have known him as a sage, a wise man. To the Celts, Merlin symbolized wisdom.

Not much is known about him. According to Geoffrey of Monmouth, Merlin was the child of the Princess of Demetia and an incubus, who seduced the princess while she was asleep. Robert de Boron, writing about A.D. 1200, wrote that a group of devils thought up a plan to create a half-human, half-demon Antichrist. Fortunately, a priest intervened and the woman chosen to bear the child was blessed. Consequently, although Merlin was born with the gift of prophecy, he was basically good.[6] His childhood was an unhappy one.

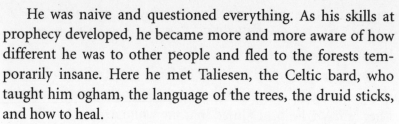

He was naive and questioned everything. As his skills at prophecy developed, he became more and more aware of how different he was to other people and fled to the forests temporarily insane. Here he met Taliesen, the Celtic bard, who taught him ogham, the language of the trees, the druid sticks, and how to heal.

Geoffrey of Monmouth, in his *History of the Kings of Britain*, describes many of Merlin's prophecies. Unfortunately, because they were written hundreds of years later, many could have been written with the benefit of hindsight.[7]

Geoffrey's book is a fascinating mixture of fact and fiction. One of his stories recounts how Merlin magically transported Stonehenge from Ireland. Apparently, King Ambrosius wanted to erect a monument on Salisbury Plain to commemorate some nobles who had been killed by the Saxons. He consulted Merlin, who suggested that they transport a circle of stones from Ireland known as the Giant's Ring. Merlin sailed to Ireland accompanied by a party of Britons that included Uther, brother of King Ambrosius, who later became father of King Arthur. Merlin dismantled the circle by magic and the stones were transported to England by ship. Merlin then cast another spell to reerect the stones over the graves of the nobles. Although this story is obviously fantasy, Geoffrey did correctly record that the stones were transported across the sea from the right direction.

There are a number of accounts of the end of Merlin's life. According to some sources he, and nine bards, went to live in a glass castle on the Isle of Bardsey with the Thirteen Treasures of Britain[8] and was not seen again. Another story claims that he was buried alive under a mountain by a young woman named Vivilian who learned her magic from him. He is still there, and his calls for help can sometimes be heard. Yet another account has both Merlin and Vivilian living happily ever after in Fairyland. Still another story has Merlin and eleven companions departing in a boat on a sea of glass. One of the triads records this as one of the Three Great Losses of Wales.

CHAPTER FIVE

Sky Stones

D ivination with stones was popular with the Celts. The Celts believed in the consciousness of all things, and even stones were thought to have a spirit. Consequently, in Celtic mythology, *Lia Fáil*, the Stone of Destiny, was able to roar with joy when it felt the touch of the rightful ruler's foot.[1] The early Christian church did not approve of stone worship, and the Synod of Arles in A.D. 452 denounced those who "venerate trees and wells and stones." Charlemagne also forbad such veneration. However, it is interesting to note that the famous Black Stone of Pergamos was brought to Rome in A.D. 205 because the Sibylline Books predicted that whoever owned it would achieve victory. Even today the British monarch is crowned on a chair containing the Stone of Scone. This dates back to Saxon times when kings were crowned on sacred stones.[2] Some people claim that the Stone of Scone was the ancient *Lia Fáil* of Irish mythology. Edward I stole this stone from the Scots in 1296, which was, in effect, an attempt to steal the sovereignty of Scotland. The Scots stole it back in 1951, but it was returned in time for the coronation of Queen Elizabeth II because she was the rightful ruler of Scotland.

Sky stones were probably named after meteorites.[3] The ancient Celts were familiar with these, and they must have been awestruck when these apparently divine symbols landed on the earth.

A popular form of divination was to toss marked stones into a fire and then try to find them again the next day. It was a sign of good luck to find the stone again. Failing to find it meant misfortune and was sometimes regarded as being a death omen.

Sky Stone divination was recorded in *The Books of Fferyllt,* one of the ancient texts of Wales. The *Fferyllt* outlined several forms of divination, but the sky stones are the most practical for today.[4]

Sky stones are easy to obtain and use and are also extremely accurate. Their limitation is that they provide only "yes" or "no" answers. Because of this, they are often referred to as "Yes-No Stones." To begin with, tossing sky stones may seem overly simplistic. Give them a try and you will quickly discover the power, energy, and accuracy they possess.

The Stones

Three stones are required: one each of gold, silver, and black. The simplest method is to find three small stones and paint them the required colors. I have done this in the past and found them highly effective, but it is much more powerful to go to a gem or rock shop and buy the correct stones.

Hematite is ideal for the silver stone, gold pyrite or tiger eye for the gold one, and obsidian for the black one. My stones are about an inch in diameter, and I keep them in a small, blue velvet bag.

My younger son used three marbles to create his own set of sky stones. Because he did not have a silver or gold marble, he substituted yellow for the gold and blue for the silver. He uses them regularly with excellent results.

The stones symbolize the three thresholds of dawn (gold), dusk (silver), and midnight (black).

Using the Stones

The simplest way of using the stones is to ask a question that can be answered by "yes" or "no." Take a few deep breaths while thinking of the question and then gently toss the three stones onto a flat surface. If you are emotionally involved in the outcome, ask someone else to toss the stones while you silently ask the question.

The stone that is closer to the black stone after they have been tossed provides the answer. If the gold stone is nearer, the answer is "yes," indicating a positive outcome. If the silver stone is closer than the gold, the answer is "no," a negative outcome. If the two stones are an equal distance away from the black stone, they need to be tossed again.

It is important to accept the answer given. Do not keep on tossing the stones in the hope of getting the opposite answer. The stones do not like being doubted and will lose effectiveness when used in this way.

Your Personal Oracle Tree

The Celts were aware of the personality in every tree. They believed that trees bridged heaven and earth and could consequently act as mediators between man and the gods. Every clan had their own personal sacred tree, which was usually sited in the middle of their territory. It was devastating when a rival clan destroyed the tree. Often this was the sole purpose of the raid, because it was so demoralizing to the enemy.

The Books of Fferyllt outlined a system of using the Sky Stones with an oracle tree, emphasizing the close relationship the Celts found between wood and stone. The easiest way to find your own personal oracle tree is to experiment by hugging trees that appeal to you. You may need to hug dozens before you find one that responds and seems to communicate with you. Do not be embarrassed at the idea of hugging a tree. Hug it in exactly the same way you would hug an old friend, and then wait for a response.

Do not try to hug every tree you come across. Hug only the ones that look aesthetically pleasing to you. It is interesting that a tree that appeals to you immensely will be ignored by a friend, who may choose a tree that you found quite unappealing. It is a very personal choice between the person and the tree. In my experience, older trees respond much better than young ones. I have also found that some trees appear to be shy and respond only when they are alone with you. Several times I have found trees that responded wonderfully well to my hug, yet appeared lifeless when I brought friends to see them. As a result, I now seek trees in remote locations and always keep the identity of the tree to myself.

It is better, anyway, to find a tree where you will not be disturbed while using your sky stones.

It is interesting to speculate whether you choose your oracle tree or if it chooses you. A number of times I have "found" an oracle tree, and over a period of time it asked me to become the guardian for an area around the tree. I have always taken these requests seriously and looked after the area the tree requested. Did the tree deliberately choose me because the area needed looking after? If your tree asks you to become a guardian, you are obligated to use your nurturing and intuitive skills to do all you can for every living thing in the area. The entire area will respond and become a special, magical place for you.

It is interesting to note that the oracle at Dodona in Greece, which rivaled Delphi in ancient times (about 800 B.C.), was situated in an ancient oak forest. The priests and priestesses at Dodona "listened" to the sounds of the ancient trees and interpreted them. The oracle came from the breeze in the branches and was magnified by bronze vessels which vibrated in the wind. This led to a popular saying, *Khalkos Dodones*, "Brass of Dodona," which meant someone who talked all the time but essentially said nothing.[5] The first mention of Dodona is in the writings of Homer, who wrote that the priestesses never washed their feet and slept on the ground.[6] These priestesses were known as "the Old Ladies" or "the Pigeons."[7] This was a reminder of an ancient legend about a pigeon which flew from Thebes in Egypt. It had rested on the oak tree and began speaking with a human voice, demanding that the oracle be instituted.[7]

Nigel Pennick records that in the middle of the grove of trees stood a single tree that had been singled out by an Egyptian princess.[8] This sacred oak must certainly have been an oracle tree. Sacred oak trees were found in many countries. The famous Oak of Meonim in Israel was called the "oak which giveth oracles." By finding your own personal oracle tree you are carrying on a very ancient tradition.

Sky Stone/Oracle Tree Divination

Now that you have your tree, decide on a good time to ask your question. Some trees prefer early morning, others like dusk. Likewise, some trees prefer a pleasant, sunny day, while others are perfectly happy to help you in the middle of a snowstorm. Your intuition will guide you to the right time.

Give your tree a good hug and ask it to act on your behalf by bringing the higher powers to your aid. Sit quietly as close to the tree as you can and meditate for a while. Recite the incantation of Amairgen. Think about your question and why you want it answered. When the time seems right, close your eyes, roll the stones around in your hand, and then gently toss them. Repeat this only if the gold and silver stones are the same distance away from the black one.

Afterwards, no matter what the answer is, give the tree another hug and thank it for its help.

The druids used their Sky Stones for other purposes as well. They would hold them while reciting triads, fingering one stone for each section.

The three stones represent the three thresholds of dawn, dusk, and midnight, all times when it is easier to cross over into the Otherworlds. The druids felt that having these stones on their person gave them confidence and greater affinity with the elements of nature.

The stones were also used with novitiates to teach them how to travel astrally. While the student was asleep, a teacher would hide the three stones nearby. The student would travel in his sleep and determine where each stone lay.[9]

Saxon Wands

The Saxon wands of Northern Europe are similar to the Sky Stones in that, in their simplest form, they also give a yes or no answer. The Saxon wands consist of seven rods of wood, four long and three short. One of the longer rods is carved or painted to distinguish it from the others. This rod, known as the Master Rod, is placed on the ground with the ends indicating north and south. This orientation is known as the Sacred Axis. The other rods are held loosely in the hand, some twelve inches above the Master Rod. The question that needs to be answered is thought about and then all the rods, except for one, are allowed to trickle out of the hand. If more long rods than short ones are on the ground the outcome is positive. Naturally, three short rods and two long ones indicate a negative outcome. If some of the rods are resting on the others and not touching the ground, the answer is uncertain. If any rod is in contact with the Master Rod, the wands do not wish to provide an answer. Finally, if the dropped sticks land pointing toward the Master Rod, the person asking the question will be able to resolve the matter using his or her own good judgment. If the sticks end up parallel to the Master Rod, the answer is up to the Fates to decide. It is also important which side of the Master Rod the sticks are on. If the majority of the sticks are on the east side, the ultimate outcome, no matter what the other interpretations may say, will be positive. Conversely, if the majority land on the west side, the final outcome will be in doubt. Like the Romans and the Greeks, the druids regarded east as being 'lucky' in their divinations.

Some authorities claim that the Saxon Wands gradually evolved into the Druid Sticks, which we will be looking at in Chapter Fourteen.[10] It is interesting to note that the Roman writer Tacitus outlined the identical procedure of divination using sticks when describing Germanic tribes, as can be found in the Irish story *Tachmarc Etain*. The procedure was to cut wands of wood and carve a script on them. After they had been tossed the resulting arrangement was interpreted.[11] The oghams and the Druid Sticks which we will be looking at shortly, like the Saxon Wands, can be used in exactly this way.

CHAPTER SIX

Touchstones

Celtic mythology contains many references to special stones. A good example is the *Lia Fáil,* commonly known as the Stone of Destiny, which was brought to this world from the Otherworld city of Falias by the Gods. Today, there are two stones that claim to be the original *Lia Fáil.* One of these is a twelve-foot-high stone on the Hill of Tara in Ireland, and the other is the Stone of Scone in the coronation chair at Westminster Abbey.[1] The mythological *Lia Fáil* screamed when Conn stood on it. When he asked his druids about it, they deliberated for fifty-three days before telling him that the stone came from the Isle of Fal and that the number of shrieks it gave indicated the number of kings that would succeed Conn.[2]

Druid rituals have always involved stones. Pliny recorded how Emperor Claudius had a Gallic knight executed for carrying a serpent stone during a trial. He then went on to explain how a serpent stone was made from the saliva and sweat of a mass of intertwined snakes. The stone was thrown up from the writhing snakes and had to be caught in a piece of cloth. The owner then had to escape quickly before the snakes realized what had happened. Serpent stones were reputed to be able to float upstream.

Stones were used to cure afflictions of all sorts. One stone might cure diseases of the joints, another would cure stomach problems. There were stones that could cure animals and stones that would encourage growth in plants.

The druids were well aware of the healing powers of different colors and would give a patient stones of specific colors to hold depending on the nature of the illness. Until a hundred years ago, it was common in Scotland for a black stone to be taken from a stream just after midnight and given to a patient suffering from mumps. A green stone obtained the same way was rubbed on the legs of people suffering with hip problems.

The Talvan Stone and *Men-an-Tol* in Cornwall are prehistoric megaliths with a hole through them. The holes were regarded as circles of power. Until recently, sick children were passed through these holes to effect a cure. *Men-an-Tol* was also known as the Crick Stone, because it was believed to be beneficial for people with a "crick in the neck."[3]

There were also "curse stones," which had to be kept in a jar of water to neutralize their power. It was believed that you could send curses to your enemy while holding the stone. Curse stones were invariably ugly, with rough surfaces. The only curse stone I have seen looked like a piece of scoria. It was kept in a jar full of water in the living room of a man I knew in Glasgow. This man would not tell me if he had ever used the stone, but I believe he did because of the sequence of tragedies that befell him. I cannot imagine any good coming to someone who keeps a curse stone in his or her home.

The remedy for someone who had been cursed was to put four colored stones into a container of water and then wash the body with this water. The stones used were black, white, red, and green.

The most important stones to the druids were the ones that could be used for divination. They could be any shape or size, but stones that contained streaks of color were especially prized.[4] Some of the touchstones that have survived have a hole through them. It is not known what this was for, but up until two hundred years ago witches apparently pushed their tongues through the hole before making their predictions.

It was not possible to find a suitable divination stone by going out and searching for one. Rather, it would find you. Consequently, if you wish to try this form of divination for yourself you will need to simply be aware of stones everywhere you go. Sooner or later—and sooner, if the stones want to work through you—a stone will attract your attention. Take it home and wash it in pure rainwater. Let it dry in the sun and then meditate with it. Close your eyes, holding the stone between your palms and see what comes to you.

You may have to meditate with it several times before it starts to speak to you. You will suddenly realize that you "know" certain things, that you have more insight into problems and difficulties that confused you before. Once you reach this stage, you can use your stone as a touchstone.

It is possible that someone will give you a touchstone when the time is right. It is reputed that Coinneach Odhar, the sixteenth-century Brahan Seer, was given his touchstone by his mother when he was seven. She in turn had been given the stone by a ghost. This stone was translucent, almost like glass, and contained streaks of bright color. Coinneach's ability to foretell the future with his touchstone led eventually to his death at the stake.[5] It is said that he tossed his touchstone into Loch Ussie shortly before his death.

A more mundane example of someone being given a touchstone was told to me some years ago by a rune master who had been given his stone by a small girl playing in the street. Her mother called her home, and she thrust the stone she had been playing with into his hand before she ran home.

Divining With Your Touchstone

Divining with a touchstone is a form of clairvoyance, closely related to psychometry. Ask the person you are reading for to hold the touchstone between the palms of his or her hands for a few minutes.

Take the stone back and hold it gently between your palms. Do not analyze anything. Simply open your mouth and say everything that comes into your mind. You will probably amaze yourself the first few times with the quantity of information that comes out. Do not concern yourself with the quality of the information for your first dozen readings. Your skills will develop markedly once you become used to your touchstone.

After each reading, wash your touchstone in rainwater and let it dry naturally, preferably in the sun.

You can use your touchstone for guidance whenever you wish. You may like to carry it around with you so you can use it wherever you happen to be. Simply relax and meditate with the touchstone between the palms of your hands. If you have a specific question, ask it, but do not insist on an answer. Sometimes the stone will not want to provide information. If you do not have a specific question, simply meditate and see what comes to you. The touchstone is particularly useful for people searching for a sense of direction.

Divining With Two Touchstones

After you have become familiar with your touchstone, you are likely to chance upon another stone that appears to be your stone's twin. Again, you will not find this by searching, but will happen upon it when you are least expecting to.

This stone is not to be given to other people to hold. You treat it in exactly the same way as the first one, cleansing it in rainwater and allowing it to dry naturally.

While your client is holding your first touchstone, hold the second one between the palms of your hands and consciously relax as much as you can. You will start to gain impressions about your sitter and the matters concerning him or her. You may even see the person's relatives and ancestors. This information can then be used in the course of the reading.

CHAPTER SEVEN

Bodhran Drum Divination

Ritual drumming is a highly effective form of magic which is often used in the shamanistic tradition. The rhythmic drumbeat has a profound effect upon the senses and emotions of all the participants. In the Celtic tradition the beat is provided by the Bodhran drum.[1]

The Celts enjoyed all forms of physical activity, and dancing was particularly popular. We do not know all of the musical instruments they had, but they certainly used the lyre or harp, a horn, the bodhran or animal-skin drum, and two sticks of wood, known as claves, which were struck together to make a rhythm.[2] Celtic music has become extremely popular again, thanks partly to the work of Enya, Clannad, and the Chieftans.

This interesting method of divination involves a round, flat drum. The wood for the frame was traditionally cut on Whitsunday and then covered with an animal skin. The drum frame was painted, and nine directional indicators were marked on the skin. When used for divination purposes the drum was held flat on one hand and between nine and twenty-one seeds of the thorn apple were dropped onto the skin. The skin was then gently tapped with a specially prepared ritual hammer, causing the

seeds to scatter on the surface. The answer to a question was determined by the relationship of the seeds to the directional indicators. Originally, earth was dropped on the drum, but because this was frequently difficult to read, seeds quickly replaced the earth.

Making the Drum

It is best to make your drum from wood, though other materials can be used if necessary. My first drum was made from a crochet hoop and worked very well. I have also made drums from cardboard and metal.

Your drum should be eight to twelve inches in diameter and three to four inches deep. My crochet hoop was less than an inch deep, which made it difficult to decorate. Rather than create a Celtic design, I contented myself with carving some oghams on it. Give some thought to the type of design you want on your drum. You may want to use some traditional Celtic designs, or perhaps draw something that relates just to you. It makes no difference as long as you are happy with the finished drum.

Traditionally, an animal skin was used for the surface of the drum. You may wish to obtain a hide and make the drum in a traditional manner. I chose canvas for mine, because the texture and springiness of it were similar to a skin, and no animal had to be killed to make my drum.

It was easy to attach the canvas to my crochet hoop drum, because the second hoop held it firmly in place. Since then, I have dampened the canvas and spread it firmly over the drum, attaching it with small tacks. I then use heavy twine around the circumference of the drum to hold it in place. As the canvas dries, it tightens, creating a firm surface.

Once it has dried, the nine directional indicators can be drawn on the canvas and the drum is ready for use.

I do not have a ritual hammer as such, preferring to use an eight inch piece of wood taken from a branch that fell from my oracle tree. Finally, you need a handful of seeds. I use twenty-one apple pips that have been dried and varnished. You will find

Bodhran Drum

it useful to prepare a large supply of seeds, because you will lose some each time you use the drum.

Divining with the Bodhran Drum

It is preferable to use the drum out of doors in a pleasant spot where you will not be disturbed. I generally sit beside my oracle tree. You may wish to do the same, or perhaps choose another attractive location, possibly in the center of a small grove of trees. You will get better results if you go to the same place each time.

Sit down comfortably and meditate for a while. Gradually formulate the exact words of your question. Once they are clear in your mind, take the apple pips in your right hand and drop them onto the drum (held in your left hand) from a height of about six inches. A few may drop off the edge of the drum, but this does not matter.

Take three deep breaths, ask your question out loud, and then tap the center of the drum firmly with your hammer or drumstick. The pips will bounce in the air and resettle. Make sure that you keep the drum as motionless as possible.

The final arrangement of the pips can now be interpreted. The Sky Stones gave either a "yes" or "no" answer. The drum doubles this. If at least three of the seeds land between the four main indicators, the outcome is deemed to be favorable. If at least two seeds finish between the top indicator and the middle one, the outcome is said to be excellent for a woman. Likewise, if two end between the middle indicator and the bottom one, the outcome is said to bode well for a man. However, if most of the seeds end up outside the main lines, the outcome is said to be unfavorable.

This method can sometimes give answers that are difficult to understand. For instance, some years ago I asked, "Will my brother-in-law win an overseas trip?" He worked for an international company who sent their top salespeople to an annual convention in an exotic location. My brother-in-law was in the running to receive one. The drum told me that the outcome was favorable to a woman, which did not seem to answer the question. However, a few weeks later my brother-in-law won the trip and the company decided my sister could accompany him.

The Bodhran drum is easy to use. Make your drum as attractive as possible. Use it only for serious questions. You will be pleasantly surprised at how attached to it you will become and how useful it will be.

St. Patrick's Drum

St. Patrick, the patron saint of Ireland, is reputed to have used a drum to eliminate all the snakes from Ireland.[3] This was just one of the many miracles attributed to him.

When he visited different parts of the country he would announce his presence by beating a large brass drum. He told everyone that he would use this drum to get rid of all the snakes. He climbed Croagh Patrick, a mountain later named after him, beating his drum as he went. Unfortunately, he beat the drum so hard that it burst. A black snake appeared and seemed to laugh as it slithered down the hillside. Many of the spectators felt that St. Patrick had promised more than he could deliver. However, an angel suddenly appeared and touched the drum, causing it to become whole again. St. Patrick started beating it again and all the snakes disappeared, never to return.

CHAPTER EIGHT

Wind Divination

The druids believed everything was created from five elements. These are fire, earth, air, water, and *nwyvre*. Nwyvre is the life force. Trees, of course, are planted in the earth and derive water from it. They reach up into the air and, being alive, also contain nwyvre. If a tree is hit by lightning, it can also often contain the element of fire. One of the reasons trees were venerated was because they are capable of having all five of the elements.

The winds were believed to carry special properties that affected all living things. Each of the four winds had a special character that could be interpreted. The divination methods of the druids have been lost in time, but a considerable lore of folk knowledge about the weather has grown up over the years, and this is believed to have derived from the druids.

A child born when the north wind was blowing would eventually receive gold, but would have to fight for it. There was a distinct possibility of injury occurring during the quest. He or she would ultimately triumph, but would have to experience defeat first.

A child born when the east wind was blowing would become prosperous and wealthy. He or she would be astute, hard-working, and easy to get along with.

A child born when the south wind was blowing would possess musical talents and an empathy with fruit and honey. This child's path through life would be smooth, and he or she would work in the fields of music, orchards, or beekeeping. He or she would enjoy a comfortable life.

A child born when the west wind was blowing would have to work hard but would never lack for food or clothing. This child would ultimately make a living from fishing, baking, or clothing.

The poor child born when no wind was blowing was likely to be a fool.

Predictions based on the weather are likely to be based on keen observation as much as prognostication. In Welsh folklore dark circles around the sun or moon were an indication of approaching winds. Other signs of wind included a red rainbow, cats sitting with their backs to the fire, and dogs chasing their tails.[1]

Part of the winter solstice ceremony of Alban Arthuan was a divination based on whichever way the wind was blowing. If it came from the north, the weather would be cold and damp; from the east, there would be snow on the hills; from the south, there would be plenty of fruit on the trees; and from the west, there would be an abundance of fish and bread.

The weather provided many methods of divination and reflected a natural interest in how the weather would affect the crops. The earth and the elements naturally governed the Celtic world, and it was natural for them to talk to the elements, thanking them for good weather and pleading for benevolence. The wind, fog, thunder, and rain were all portents that could be interpreted.

A sunny January meant a bad February and March. Snow in January meant the soil would be well fed. A sunny February meant the rest of the year would be bad. Bad weather that month killed off the pigs. A windy March indicated good crops. A good start to the month indicated a wet finish, and vice-versa. A cold April was excellent for the hay. A dry April indicated a mediocre summer. Plenty of flowers in April meant a shortage of apples and plums. A cold May was good for hay and also meant fewer deaths than usual. A warm June was good for crops and the hives. Rain on the second day of July meant the rest of the month would be wet. A swarm of bees in July indicated a difficult winter. If August began with misty weather, it would be hot before the month was over. If the first day of September was dry, the rest of the month would be also. A sunny October indicated a wet winter. Bad weather in early November meant winter would start early and last late. Frost in December before Christmas meant winter would be mild. If Christmas Day was green, Easter would be white.

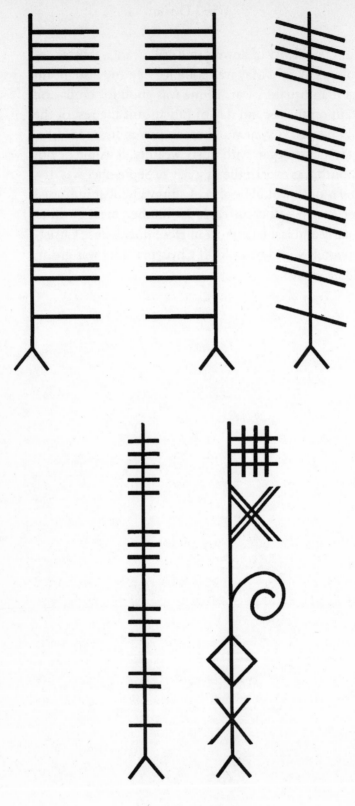

The Ogham Alphabet

CHAPTER NINE

The Oghams

The Celts credit Taut, one of their gods, for the invention of writing. Although the druids chose not to write down their secrets, they wrote messages in Greek, and they also used the ogham alphabet and a system of tree-writing known as *bobileth*. Tree-writing used an alphabet of thirty-four letters each represented by a different tree. A message was constructed by stringing various leaves on a cord, with each leaf representing a different letter. This same principle was used by the ancient Peruvians and can also be related to the wampum belts worn by Native Americans. We inherited the term "leaves" of a book from the ancient Celtic *bobileth*.

There was also a bardic alphabet, known as the oghams. The oghams were composed of single strokes cut across a line or on the corner of a stone or wooden object. Each ogham is a mnemonic that relates first to a tree, and then to a variety of plants, animals, and other objects. Ogham is pronounced *ohm*, a name used around the world to signify God.

Several hundred ogham inscriptions still survive, the majority (about 360) carved in stone. Some three hundred of these are

in Southern Ireland, and the remainder are scattered around the British Isles.[1]

The first oghams I ever saw were in Lewannick, Cornwall. In this quiet place, a few miles south of Launceston, is an old church. At the time I was keen on brass rubbing and stopped here in the hope of finding a suitable brass. I was disappointed in this regard, but my visit became an unforgettable one as an elderly parishioner showed me their ogham stones. Safely preserved inside the church is a memorial stone with the inscription "Here lies Ulcagnus" written in Latin as well as ogham. Out in the churchyard is a second ogham stone, with the inscription "To the memory of Incenvus." This second stone is badly worn, which is not surprising, because it has been exposed to the elements for almost two thousand years.

The ogham letters appear to have been used originally to record inscriptions on stone or wood. Large wooden tablets were usually cut from yew trees at definite, prescribed times. Other sacred woods were used when yew was not available. In time these wooden tablets evolved into large, wooden books that were opened like a fan.

The ogham alphabet is reputed to have been devised by Ogma (also known as Ogmas), son of King Elathan, around 600 B.C. as proof of his ingenuity.[2] However, the oldest surviving inscriptions in ogham date back only to the fourth century A.D. This is not surprising, as it is the corners of stones that are most vulnerable to damage. The ogham script never entirely disappeared and was carefully studied by historians in the Middle Ages. Ogham faded from use about A.D. 650.[3] In the early 1600s the Earl of Glamorgan used ogham to secretly communicate with Charles I of England. A hundred years later the Celtic revival began, engendering new interest in the ogham alphabet.

The letters were symbolic, with each letter indicating a wide variety of ideas relating to Celtic philosophy. In effect, it was a secret code, kept from the common man and widely used by the learned. Ogma specifically wanted to keep the ogham letters away from the "farmers and herdsmen" and "the vulgar and poor of the nation." Irish legends tell of whole libraries written in ogham where all the ancient stories were preserved. More often, though, ogham was used to write magic spells.[4]

The basic alphabet consists of twenty-five letters. It is believed that Ogma invented the first twenty letters and that the last five, representing the diphthongs, were a much later addition. The Irish name for the last five letters is *forfedha,* which means additional letter. The last five letters have not been found on any pre-medieval inscriptions.

The letters can be grouped in a variety of ways, but the most usual method is to sort them into five groups of five. Another popular method, using twenty-six letters, is to sort them into three groups of eight, like the Futhark runes, and have two left over.

An earlier system, known as the "Ladder of Learning," used twenty-four letters, sorted into four groups of five plus four additional letters. A young student would start on the first letter and gradually progress through the alphabet. Each letter was regarded as being one rung on a ladder and related to a specific lesson the student was working on. This is why it often took students twenty years to learn all the mysteries of druidism. In addition to the twenty main rungs of the ladder, there was an unnamed rung and three intermediary rungs, called "Quests of Mastery."

The ogham letters provided a complete system for classifying the entire universe the Celts lived in. The letters were not simply an alphabet, such as we have today, but rather a complete cosmological system. The conscious decision not to write down their mysteries made it vital that the druids have a complex mnemonic system to remember their teachings. The ogham alphabet provided this system.

The ogham alphabet, with each letter so replete with information, evolved naturally into a system of divination. The druids took divination seriously and used a wide variety of methods to determine the future. It was never performed as an entertainment or parlor game. Consequently, their systems of divination are rather different to many modern methods of "fortunetelling." They used divination techniques to learn the hidden secrets about things, so they could be just as interested

in divining someone's secret past as in determining the future. They understood that by knowing someone's past, the future can be predicted with a great deal of precision.

CHAPTER TEN

Meanings of the Oghams

Each ogham relates primarily to a tree, which is then in turn related to a color, animal, and tree month. As shown on the following pages, the Celts had a wide variety of items that could be connected with each ogham, allowing a single tree to act as a mnemonic for a large number of apparently unconnected objects.

Beithe—Birch

Keyword: Beginnings
Color: White
Animal: Cow
Tree Month: December 24–January 20

The graceful, white-stemmed birch with its beautiful green leaves represents the Otherworld. In medieval romances, a woman with pure white skin dressed in green is someone from the Otherworld. The birch tree protects women from being taken to the Otherworld. Maypoles are traditionally made from birch, and in Wales living, standing trees were used. Beithe relates to the Gaelic words *bith* (enduring) and *bithe* (womanly). Festival fires were usually oak, but birch was used for kindling at Beltaine. The birch tree is traditionally the very first tree to have had an ogham letter carved on it.

Beithe represents the start of the Celtic year, which is held on November 1st—Samhaine. Consequently, Beithe represents new starts, making plans, and a major step forward. It is important to get rid of outworn ideas and negative influences to allow progress to take place. In the modern calendar, the first Celtic month is Beithe, which lasts from December 24th to January 20th. The Celtic year consists of thirteen lunar months.

Pliny reported that rods made of birch were used by magistrates and school teachers. Until recently, criminals on the Isle of Man were birched to drive out the evil forces that bedeviled them. Beithe has the power to eliminate negative energies.

Beithe has always been regarded as an indicator of good fortune, luck, and change. Most people fear change, and Beithe provides the challenge of mastering life in a state of flux. This change could relate to travel.

Luis—Rowan

Keyword: Insight
Color: Red and Gray
Animal: Unicorn and Bear
Tree Month: January 21–February 17

The rowan tree was important to the Druids. Before going into battle, they would say incantations over fires made from rowan wood. The rowan tree was often called "the Lady of the Mountain" or "the Tree of Life." It also bears the name *fid na nDruad,* the "Druids tree." In ancient times groves of rowan trees could be found at sacred sites. As recently as two hundred years ago, John Lightfoot, in *Flora Scotica,* mentioned that rowan trees were frequently found close to stone circles in Scotland. The rowan berry contains a pentagram, the ancient sign of protection, opposite the stalk. It was believed that a cross made of rowan would preserve the owner from misfortune.

It is not surprising then that Luis represents protection and the ability to distinguish good from bad. It provides foreknowledge about events outside ourselves that could be damaging. It is a sign that the person has sufficient energy and stamina to overcome the potential difficulties.

The challenge of Luis is conquering self-doubt. It can also indicate that you are facing psychic attack, but will not be harmed if you take precautions.

LUIS

ROWAN

Fearn—Alder

Keyword: Strength
Color: Crimson
Animal: Red Fox, Ram, and Stallion
Tree Month: February 18–March 17

Alder is a water-resistant wood used by the ancient Celts to build underwater foundations for their lake dwellings in what is now known as Switzerland. The wood takes longer to rot than virtually any other tree, so it was also used for water wheels, canal gates, and any other purpose where it would be in contact with water. Winchester Cathedral was built on piles of alder.

Alder was the sacred tree of Bran, the Celtic god-king, whose head was finally buried where the Tower of London was later built, after being an oracle for many years. Alder is a white wood, but its sap is red, giving it a fiery energy.

This energy gives strength, both moral and physical. It is an indication to remain true to oneself and not to be compromised. The danger is that you may become stubborn and resistant to change.

The challenge is to know when to move forward and when to consolidate.

ALDER

Saille—Willow

Keyword: Intuition
Color: *Sorcha,* Fiery
Animal: Hare and Cat
Tree Month: March 18–April 14

Saille represents the subconscious, feminine, and mystical side of our natures. It relates to the moon and fertility. The Celts held women in higher esteem than is sometimes the case today. Male and female were different, but equal. There were many druidess schools, famous for producing gifted clairvoyants. Saille has become anglicized into "Sally." Hence the song, "Sally Gardens." The Celts believed that God made the human spine from the willow.

Saille relates to intuition, creativity, and imagination. Its effects are more powerful at night when the moon is out. It can sometimes relate to self-deception. It is an indication that someone not yet known to you (but probably a woman) will teach you something that you need to know.

The challenge of Saille is not to ignore the intuitive and spiritual side of your nature.

SAILLE

WILLOW

Nuin—Ash

Keyword: Peace
Color: Clear Green
Animal: Snake
Tree Month: April 15–May 12

The ash has always been regarded as a magical tree. Three of the five sacred trees of Eirinn were ashes (the other two were oak and yew). Medicines have been produced from it, and in Celtic cosmology it encompasses all three circles of existence, linking this world with the Otherworlds. The broomstick was at one time used for divination. Traditionally, the staff was made from ash. The twigs came from birch, hazel, and rowan, and these were bound with willow. The broom was known as the *Dasgubell Rod*, the besom that sweeps away anything that conceals the truth. Nuin is an indication to bring your life into balance and find peace within.

The challenge is to realize that things are not always as they seem. You must learn to separate the wheat from the chaff and continually strive to become the best that you are capable of becoming.

NUIN

ASH

Huathe—Hawthorn

Keyword: Restraint
Color: Purple
Animal: Goat and Dragon
Tree Month: May 13–June 9

The hawthorn is supposed to bring bad luck to anyone who cuts it down. This traditionally meant the death of one's children or livestock, or financial ruin. In recent years, a hawthorn tree was cut down to make room for the short-lived DeLorean car factory in Northern Ireland. The locals were convinced the factory was doomed and were not surprised when it collapsed.

The hawthorn relates to two completely opposite poles of sexuality—abstinence and excess. A hawthorn that grew inside Glastonbury Abbey was cut down by the puritans, probably because of its sexual and pagan associations. This famous Glastonbury thorn is said to have come from a stick of hawthorn that Joseph of Arimathea thrust into a hill when he arrived to preach the gospel in England in A.D. 60. Fortunately, cuttings were kept from the hawthorn that Cromwell's men cut down, and it can still be seen flowering in Glastonbury in May and at Christmas time. Hawthorns can live for up to four hundred years and were believed to be the dwelling places of faerie folk.

The hawthorn indicates a time of cleansing. It is a time to be patient and grow inwardly. It provides the perfect time to think before taking action. It also relates to hope. In the time of the Crusades, departing knights would give their loves sprigs of hawthorn, so they could "live in hope."[1]

The challenge is to be patient and to make proper plans before proceeding. It relates to *festina lente,* "make haste slowly."

HAWTHORN

Duir—Oak

Keyword: Protection
Color: Dark Brown and Black
Animal: White Horse, Lion, and Salamander
Tree Month: June 10–July 7

Oak is one of the most important trees to the Celts. At one time it was thought that bards and druids could gain inspiration by eating acorns. Oak groves were regarded as sacred places by the druids, who preached and taught under their spreading branches. Oaks grow slowly, finally becoming the kings of the forest.

Oaks have been sacred trees for many civilizations. In Scandinavia the oak is related to Thor, in India to Indra, in Greece to Jupiter, and in Finland to Ukho. Ovid tells the story of Philomon asking Jupiter to turn him into an oak tree. His wife, Baukis, was turned into a linden tree.

Duir is a word meaning solidity, steadfastness, and protection. The oak represents all of these things. It also reveals a doorway to new understanding and inner spirituality. The word "door" derives from the Gaelic *duir*. Other meanings are protection from harm and strength.

The challenge is to be strong and to stand up for yourself. You may need to be tested in some way, but if you stand firm to what you believe is right Duir will give you the necessary strength and endurance.

DUIR

OAK

Tinne—Holly

Keyword: Balance
Color: Dark Gray
Animal: War Horse
Tree Month: July 8–August 4

The holly has foliage all year round. In summer it is soft, but in winter, when there is a shortage of greenery, the leaves harden and spines appear. Holly is the holy tree of Christianity, as its thorns are symbols of the crown of thorns worn by Christ. Traditionally, holly was planted close to houses to protect them from lightning and thunder.

Tinne relates to balance, fair play, and right overcoming wrong. It is a sign of justice and gives strength and power. If your cause is right, you will ultimately succeed.

The challenge is to find a suitable goal for yourself. You may have a lack of direction, or be unequipped for the task at hand.

HOLLY

Coll—Hazel

Keyword: Intuition
Color: *Cron,* Brown
Animal: Salmon
Tree Month: August 5–September 1

Hazel is associated with salmon in Celtic lore. In Celtic mythology, the nine hazels of knowledge dropped their nuts into Connla's well, giving wisdom to the salmon. Aengus, the Celtic God of Love, carried a hazel wand, and this tradition passed on to many druids and even bishops of the early Christian church. As late as the eighteenth century, people would use twigs of hazel to keep witches away from their homes.

Coll represents creativity, poetry, divination, and mediation. The creativity can either be a catalyst to inspire others, or yourself. It indicates learning and the start of knowledge and wisdom. As well as logic, intuition is enhanced by Coll.

The challenge is that you may tend to ignore your intuitive side and block your creativity. Other blockages could be caused by subconscious fears of failure.

COLL

HAZEL

Quert—Apple

Keyword: Beauty
Color: Green
Animal: Unicorn
Tree Month: September 2–29

Quert is related to Avalon, the "Isle of Apples." Glastonbury is sited in these Celtic apple lands. In the Welsh poem "Avellenau," we learn that Merlin told his lord of this secret, magical orchard. Apples have been related to Pythagoras because, if they are cut crosswise, the pips can be seen housed inside a pentagram.

Quert relates to youthfulness and beauty. It means that you should seek beauty and perfection in everything you do. You should live life to the full and make the most of every opportunity. It does not mean looking at life through "rose-colored glasses." You still need to ask questions and evaluate things carefully before acting.

The challenge of Quert is to make the right choice from a group of options. There may be a tendency to try and do too many things at the same time, diffusing your energies and limiting your chances of success.

QUERT

APPLE

Muin—Vine

Keyword: Prophecy
Color: *Mbracht,* Variegated
Animal: Lizard
Tree Month: September 30–October 27

The grapevine was introduced to the British Isles from the continent thousands of years ago. Bronze age objects were frequently decorated with the fruits and foliage of the grape. It was difficult to grow and produce grapes in Britain.

Muin indicates a release from restraints, and the ability to speak openly and honestly. Of course, a glass or two of wine can do wonders in releasing inhibitions. It allows the conscious and subconscious minds to meld and the intuitive side to surface.

The challenge is to relax and unwind when necessary. When we are overly stressed, intuition suffers. We must learn to step outside ourselves every now and again and enjoy the simple things of life.

MUIN

VINE

Gort—Ivy

Keyword: Progress
Color: Sky Blue
Animal: Boar
Tree Month: October 28–November 24

The ivy can grow almost anywhere. It is extremely hardy, is difficult to destroy, and can live to a great age. Since ancient times, the holly and ivy have been regarded as natural enemies. The carol, "The Holly and the Ivy," reflects this. The ivy leaf was part of the design of early Celtic coins.

Gort is an indication of change and progress, usually in your career. Ivy progresses in spirals, giving many opportunities to be sidetracked. Keep your eye firmly on your main goal, and Gort will help you make progress towards it.

The challenge of Gort is to avoid ruts and other pitfalls. Other people may be envious of your success and try to trip you up.

GORT

IVY

Ngetal—Reed

Keyword: Unity
Color: Grass Green
Animal: Dog, Stag, and Rat
Tree Month: November 25–December 23

The reed grows in the shallows. In the days of the druids, reeds were much more abundant than they are today, as we have drained much of the marshes and swamplands. The reeds stood tall and were caressed by the breeze. They were often associated with spiritual wisdom. Both Taliesen and Moses were found in the reeds. There is an old saying: "Oaks may fall when reeds stand in a storm." The Welsh made a type of paper known as *plagawd* from the reed. Reeds were traditionally used as measuring rods. They were also used to make thatch roofs and for floor coverings.

Ngetal is an indication of harmony between you and the rest of the world. It signifies unity of purpose and will. It gives you the ability to adapt to changing conditions. It can also signify spiritual growth.

The challenge of Ngetal is to use your talents to progress. You may suffer from doubts and anxieties and lack direction.

NGETAL

Straif—Blackthorn

Keyword: Fate
Color: Bright Purple
Animal: Wolf, Toad, and Black Cat

The blackthorn is traditionally a sign of bad luck. When allowed to grow freely, the blackthorn forms dense thickets protected with nasty thorns. The Gaelic word *straif* is related to the English "strife." Branches of blackthorn are used for making the fighting sticks known as *shillelaghs*. When witches were burned, blackthorn branches were often thrown onto the pyre. This is because it was believed that the witches' "black rod" was made from blackthorn.

Straif is an indication that things are happening that you cannot control. Unexpected changes are very difficult to handle, and you must carefully evaluate the situation to try to find a solution.

The challenge of Straif is to try to turn a negative experience into a positive one. If you are given a lemon and manage to turn it into lemonade, you will learn a great deal and be a better, stronger person as a result of this growing experience.

STRAIF

BLACKTHORN

Ruis—Elder

Keyword: Change
Color: Blood-red
Animal: Badger

The elder is a tree of regeneration. Damaged branches regrow quickly, and it will root readily from any part. The elder was regarded as being a faerie tree, and before anything was taken from it permission had to be obtained by asking the tree spirits. It was believed that if an elder tree was destroyed, the faeries would leave the farmer's property. Consequently, branches might be removed, but the tree was never cut down. In East Anglia it was considered bad luck to burn elder wood in the house. The elder is a hard wood that was frequently used for fishing rods. It was also believed that witches' broomsticks were made from elder.

Ruis relates to the cycles of change and the transition from one state to another. It represents the passing away of something to make way for the new. Change is inevitable, and it is necessary to let go of things that no longer have any bearing on your life.

The challenge of Ruis is to come to terms with the necessity for change. It is natural to want to hold on and resist change, but this should be avoided. Stagnation results if you refuse to accept change.

ELDER

Ailm—Fir

Keyword: Power
Color: Pale Blue
Animal: Red Cow

Firs are tall, slender trees standing on high hill slopes. Fir cones open up in hot weather and close again when rain is on its way. It is possible that the first Christmas trees were firs. Fir trees signify a higher, more powerful perspective.

Consequently, Ailm gives insight and the potential for great wisdom. It is an indication that you are progressing and will shortly be able to see ahead much more clearly than before. You will have more self-esteem, strength, and personal power.

The challenge is to carefully consider where you want to go before moving ahead. The tendency will be to rush in without sufficient thought.

Ohn—Furze

Keyword: Wisdom
Color: Yellow and Gold
Animal: Rabbit

Bees work hard to collect pollen and nectar, which they then take back to their hives to convert into honey. Furze, or gorse, is loved by bees and symbolizes the collecting of valuable knowledge. In many ways gorse symbolizes testing and purification. It used to be burned in the fall to encourage a new growth in the spring that the sheep could eat.

Ohn indicates that you should make use of the knowledge you already have, or acquire the necessary knowledge, to achieve wisdom and mastery.

The challenge of Ohn is to avoid scattering your energies, You must also remain aware of the ultimate goal and not become totally lost in the information-gathering stage.

OHN

FURZE

Ur—Heather

Keyword: Magnificent Obsession
Color: Purple
Animal: Bee and Lion

Heather grows readily all over Britain. Red heather is a sign of passion, while white heather acts as a protection against acts of passion. In early Celtic times mattresses were made from heather. It was also mixed with mud and straw to make walls of houses, particularly in the Scottish highlands, and to thatch roofs. A sprig of heather has always been regarded as "lucky."

Ur is an indication that you should find a "magnificent obsession" for yourself, something big, imaginative, and a true test of your abilities. You should pay attention to your dreams and intuition as you search for this worthy goal.

The challenge of Ur is to act on your dreams. Many people daydream about all the things they would like to do and be. You must act on these dreams and make them happen.

HEATHER

Eadha—Aspen

Keyword: Endurance
Color: Silver and Red
Animal: White Mare

Ancient craftsmen made shields from the aspen. Bards would often listen to the sounds of the wind rustling the leaves of the aspen before making their pronouncements. Many people believed that faeries lived in these trees and the rustling leaves were their conversation. Early Christian leaders cursed the aspen because they believed that the Cross was made from it.

Eadha is an indication that you have the necessary qualities to endure and overcome negative situations. Eadha encourages and protects you through life's difficult periods. It is a sign that you will ultimately succeed if you stick to the task.

The challenge is not to give in when events conspire against you. You may be full of doubts and fears, but you must persevere.

ASPEN

Ioho—Yew

Keyword: Immortality
Color: Dark Green
Animal: Spider

There are yew trees in Britain that are two thousand years old, making this tree a good symbol for immortality. Yews were planted around graveyards long after the original symbolism had been forgotten. Longbows and ogham staves were usually made from yew.

Ioho stands for transformation and rebirth. It symbolizes what you have inherited from your ancestral past. It gives new strength and enthusiasm and the ability to understand hidden truths.

The challenge of Ioho is to handle the feelings of loss that occur whenever a transformation takes place.

The first twenty oghams are the original ones. The last five were added much later and many purists refuse to use them for divination purposes. I have included them for completeness.

Koad—Sacred Grove

Keyword: Knowledge
Color: Green
Animal: Squirrel

Rather than a single tree, Koad represents the sacred groves that were so venerated by the Celts. These groves, which were always found near a spring, usually consisted of oak trees. The special magic of these sacred groves has always been felt by sensitive people. Consequently, Koad represents hidden knowledge being revealed, everything falling into place so that mysteries are suddenly understood.

The challenge of Koad is that you may be too single-minded and unable to see the overall picture. Step back a few paces and allow the understanding to come in.

KOAD

SACRED GROVE

Oir—Spindle

Keyword: Inner Peace and Contentment
Color: White
Animal: Owl

The spindle is a small tree that produces a hard wood traditionally used for making pegs, bobbins, and spindles.

It represents the inner peace and tranquility one finds after achieving a worthwhile goal, something difficult and challenging. It is success after achieving something that was done for its own sake, without expecting any other reward.

The challenge of Oir is that you may take life too seriously, and consequently miss the moments of peace, delight, and real happiness.

OR

SPINDLE

Uinllean—Honeysuckle

Keyword: Ancient Wisdom
Color: Pale Yellow
Animal: Mouse

It used to be believed that honeysuckle could give young women erotic dreams, so many mothers refused to allow the honeysuckle in the house. It is commonly known as "evening pride."

Uinllean is an indication that you will be able to see through situations and understand what is worthwhile and what is false. It means that you will instinctively know the right actions to take.

The challenge of Uinllean is conquering uncertainty and hesitancy. You will need to gain confidence in yourself before you can progress.

UINLLEAN

HONEYSUCKLE

Phogos—Beech

Keyword: Guidance From the Past
Color: Orange
Animal: Deer

The words "beech" and "book" have the same origin, because many writing tablets were made from this wood.

Phogos is an indication that answers can be found by examining our own pasts. Too often we repeat mistakes by not learning. Phogos tells us that it is never too late to learn and to gain guidance from the past.

The challenge of Phogos is to evaluate information carefully and not to discard things purely because they are old.

PHOGOS

BEECH

Peine—Pine

Keyword: Illumination
Color: Blue-Green
Animal: Cat

The Scots Pine produces cones that are believed to contain hidden wisdom. They used to be called "tree eggs." The Celts regarded the pine as one of their chieftain trees and equated it with heroes and warriors. The pine is also regarded as the tree of illumination, in the sense of providing the insights that reveal the way ahead.

Peine is the twenty-fifth ogham and has been given many meanings in the past. It is said to also relate to *Xi*, meaning spirit, and *Mor*, meaning sea. *Xi* relates to illumination and spiritual growth. *Mor* relates to travel, and more particularly the mystical, intuitive, feminine sides of our natures.

PINE

A Wooden Few

CHAPTER ELEVEN

Making Your Own Oghams

Divination oghams are usually made of wood, though you can make them out of any material that is pleasing to you. A friend of mine has a beautiful set of embroidered oghams which she uses. She designed and made them herself and finds them very useful. Each ogham in the set is known as a *few*.

My first oghams were made from pieces of cardboard the same size and shape as playing cards. I simply drew one ogham character on each card and made a very basic set of fews. I found this very helpful to begin with. After a while, I designed a more elaborate set with a picture on each card, which I still use from time to time.

I also made a set of wooden fews. I bought some wood used for fine trellis work and cut it into lengths about three inches long. This gave me twenty-five pieces of wood, three inches by half an inch by a quarter of an inch. Using an artist's engraving tool, it was a simple matter to carve an ogham character on each piece and create a set of oghams that I thoroughly enjoy using. I keep them in an attractive bag decorated with a Celtic design.

It would be ideal if you could create your oghams from the tree each character represents. Thus you would end up with a set where Beithe was made from a piece of Birch, Luis from Rowan,

and so on. I have made a start on this for myself, because I feel that the completed set would not only look attractive, but would be particularly powerful.

One of my students made herself a set using small lengths of green plastic. She is very happy with them and finds them highly expressive.

Another person I know made a set using small, round pebbles he found on the beach. He spent several weeks searching for pebbles of the size and shape he wanted. Using psychometry, he decided which stone would be used for each character and then painted an ogham character on each one. His set is very attractive to handle and use.

I have heard of oghams being made from silver. Recently, I saw a photograph of someone using a set of oghams made by encasing the leaves of the different trees in clear plastic. It appears that oghams can be made from almost anything.

Traditionally, oghams for divination were made from pieces of wood, and certainly my wood oghams have a feeling to them that none of the other types possess. Because they are more fun to use than my other sets, I feel I get better results with them. The oghams made from lengths of wood were called *crann-chur* in ancient Ireland and *coelbren* in Wales.

However, my friends with oghams made from other materials are happy with their choice and would not change. The best thing is to experiment and find which material is best for you.

Many ogham readers use only the first twenty characters, regarding the final five as a later addition that has no value. I find it helpful to include the extra characters, because they provide different nuances of meaning that can be very useful. Again, experiment and see what works best for you. Remember that ogham alphabets have been found that contain from eighteen characters up to thirty.

The Ogham Cloth

Your fews will have to be cast on a cloth or wooden surface. Pure white is best for the cloth, and you can mark or embroider the

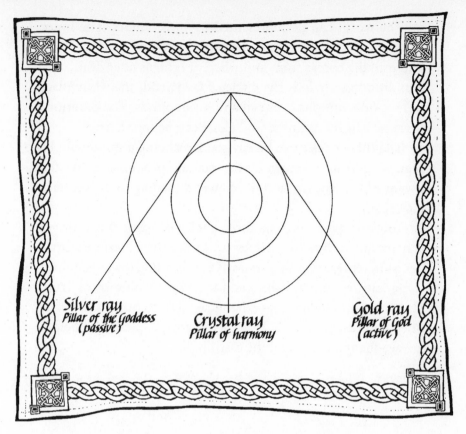

Silver ray
Pillar of the Goddess
(passive)

Crystal ray
Pillar of harmony

Gold ray
Pillar of God
(active)

The Three Circles of Annwn on Ogham Cloth

three circles of Annwn on it. My cloth is almost three feet square, and I find this a good size to use.

The Three Circles of Annwn

In Celtic cosmology, all of life can be represented by three circles of being. At the beginning of time there was nothing but God and the spirit world, known as Annwn. The world came into being when God spoke his name. The name of God was so sacred that druids were not allowed to say the name out loud to anyone other than another druid. The letters representing the name—O, I, U—could be shown to others but not spoken. These three letters were also represented by three lines, known as the Three Columns of Truth.

The world can be represented by three circles. The innermost circle, known as Abred, in the realm of matter. This is where all life comes from and where it returns after death. Surrounding this circle is the circle of Gwynedd, the white place. Here good triumphs over evil and joy abounds. The outermost circle is Ceugant, infinity. God alone can be found here.

The three circles can be envisaged as being a spiral with life beginning from Annwn in the center, progressing through Gwynned to Ceugant, and ultimately returning to the center to start again.

You may wish to draw three circles on your cloth, or you may prefer to draw two circles and have the outermost circle, Ceugant, represented by a series of rays heading towards infinity.

Finally, you may wish to add the Three Columns of Truth. This is not strictly necessary, because these columns are created when you cast your fews. However, many people find it helpful to have them included on the casting cloth.

CHAPTER TWELVE

Reading the Oghams

Now it is time to cast your ogham-fews and give yourself a reading. Find a place where you will not be disturbed. If possible, use the oghams outdoors. You may find that you get better results if you read for yourself beside your oracle tree. If circumstances do not allow, simply choose a comfortable place indoors.

We do not know how the druids read from the oghams. Many different layouts have been suggested. The one about to be described is one I devised myself and have used with excellent results for almost twenty years.

Spread your cloth and spend a few moments contemplating the three circles of Annwn. Visualize life beginning at the very center, spiralling outward, and finally returning to God.

Then take your fews and mix them in your hands. If this is awkward, mix them on the ground. Do not look at them while doing this. When the moment seems right, while still mixing the fews, say the following words of Amairgen, preferably out loud:

I am a Wind that blows over the sea;
I am a Wave of the Ocean;
I am a ray of the Sun;

I am a salmon in the Water;
I am the God that creates in the head of man the fire of
   thought.

Now think of your question and randomly select a few. Place
it at the bottom of the outermost circle (Ring of Ceugant). Take
another few and place it in the center of the three rings (inside
the Ring of Abred). The third few is placed above this at the top
of the Ring of Ceugant.

What we have done so far is create the middle column of the
Three Columns of Truth. This is known as the Pillar of Harmony.

Six more fews are selected at random and placed in position,
creating the remaining two columns. The left hand column is
called the Pillar of the Goddess, and the right hand one is the
Pillar of God. We start with the bottom few of the Pillar of the
Goddess, followed by the bottom few of the Pillar of God. The
middle fews are placed in position in the same order, followed
by the top ones.

We now have nine fews on the casting cloth. Nine is a spiritual number, but, more importantly, we have three triads: the
bottom three, representing the past; the middle three, covering
the present; and the top three, which look into the future.[1]

Interpreting the Spread

We can look at the results in a number of ways. We can look at the
fews as three triads, one each for the past, present, and future. We
could look at the three fews in the middle column (the Pillar of
Harmony) and see the past, present, and future. We should also
look at the Pillar of the Goddess and see the hidden, possibly over-
looked situations behind the past, present, and future. Also, we
can look at the fews in the Pillar of God and see the things that we
should have done in the past and can do in the present and future.

Let's look at a reading I gave for a neighbor recently. Gloria's
question was, "Will I be promoted from my present position at
work?" She was secretary to the manager of a printing company.
When she had been hired two years earlier, her boss had
promised that she would be promoted to a sales representative

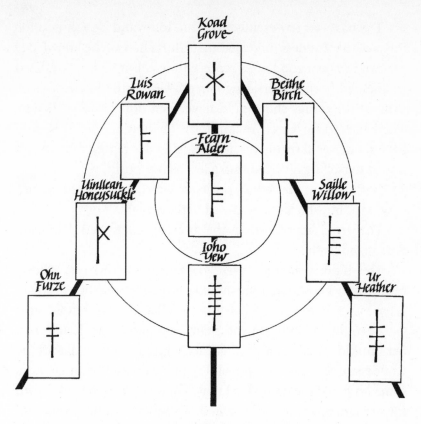

Koad
Grove

Luis
Rowan

Beithe
Birch

Fearn
Alder

Uinllean
Honeysuckle

Saille
Willow

Ioho
Yew

Ohn
Furze

Ur
Heather

A Sample Reading

position as soon as a vacancy occurred. Two opportunities had arisen over the two years, but in each case her boss had hired someone from outside the company.

As I was doing the reading for Gloria, I had her mix the fews and pass them to me to place on the cloth.

I began by looking at the Pillar of Harmony, because this gave me a quick assessment of the matter. The past was represented by Ioho. This indicated that accepting the position two years earlier had represented a whole new start for Gloria. Fearn, in the center, showed that she was going to stick to her principles and not allow herself to be pushed around by anyone. The future was represented by Koad. This was positive, indicating that Gloria would soon understand why the promotion had been so long delayed.

Now that I knew the outcome was positive, I began looking at Gloria's spread triad by triad.

The past was represented by Ohn, Ioho, and Ur. Ohn on the Pillar of the Goddess indicated that Gloria had all the knowledge required to be a good sales representative, but had not realized it. She had been underrating herself. Ur, on the Pillar of God, showed the things she should have been doing two years ago. The keyword for Ur is "magnificent obsession." Gloria should have set her goal firmly on becoming a sales representative and not let herself be diverted into a less senior position.

With Ioho in the central position, Gloria had indeed made a new start, but she had not aimed high enough.

The triad representing the present contained Uinllean, Fearn, and Saille.

The hidden energies were contained in Uinllean. Gloria instinctively knows what she should do, but is probably refusing to listen to her inner voice. The few in the Pillar of God showed what Gloria could do in the present. Saille showed that she should trust her intuition, making a good foil for Uinllean in the Pillar of the Goddess. It also gave the possibility of a woman teaching Gloria something that she needed to know. These two fews, coupled with the strength provided by Fearn in the Pillar of Harmony, show that if she acted on her feelings, she would be likely to get what she wants. She would have to avoid being overly stubborn, though.

Finally, the future triad: Luis, Koad, and Beithe. Luis, on the Pillar of the Goddess, provides protection and insight. It shows that Gloria will have the necessary energy to achieve her goal. It is likely that Gloria will not be aware of these things, as the few on the Pillar of the Goddess is often hidden. Nonetheless, Luis is an excellent few in this position.

Beithe, on the Pillar of God, is the very first few and represents new starts. Gloria will shortly be making a major step forward. Beithe harmonizes well with Koad in the central position. Koad shows that everything will fall into place, allowing the progressive energies of Beithe to be fully utilized.

The outcome of all this happened just a few weeks later. A sales representative resigned and Gloria assumed that she would be offered the position. This did not happen, and the position was advertised in the papers. Gloria was furious, but then had a sudden flash of insight (Koad). After she calmed down, she told her boss that she wanted the position, and reminded him of his earlier promise. He admitted that she would be ideal for the position, but as she was so good at her secretarial duties he had hoped that she might have given up her ambitions and remained as his secretary. He apologized for his selfishness and gave her the job. Gloria is enjoying her new position and is now aiming to become the sales manager.

One Ogham Reading

The oghams can be very useful in providing insight into minor problems as well. Do a proper layout as described above, when you have time. If you simply want a quick answer, mix the oghams in their bag while thinking of the question. When the moment seems right, pull one ogham out of the bag and interpret it.

Several weeks ago I wondered if I should pay a routine visit to my dentist before traveling several hundred miles to give some lectures. The ogham I selected was Nuin, which has the key word "peace." I wondered if I would have peace on the trip if I visited the dentist first, or if it would be a peaceful trip even if I delayed my visit until afterwards. When I remembered that the challenge of Nuin is that things are not always as they seem, I called my dentist and made an appointment.

Ogham Progressions

The oghams can also be used to provide insight into the months and years ahead. This can be very useful, because each individual few can represent one month. Consequently, it is possible to determine in advance the best months for different activities.

Bill has been a friend of mine for more than twenty years. He used to laugh at my interests, but he gradually became interested himself and is now an extremely good Tarot card reader. He came to me for guidance because he had some important decisions to make. He wondered if it was a good time to change location. He wanted to move to a smaller city and was worried that

he might not be able to make a reasonable living there. His intention was to leave his present job and become a full-time Tarot reader. He was also concerned that his wife was not one hundred per cent behind the idea.

"I'm so fed up with my job," he told me. "I've been there fifteen years and I'm just taken for granted. It's time I did something for myself."

I offered to give him a six-month reading with the oghams. Bill mixed the fews and selected six of them, one at a time, to indicate the next six months. I laid these out in a row in front of him. The first few Bill chose was Coll. This represented the next month. Coll means creativity and trusting your intuition.

"In the next few weeks, pay particular attention to your feelings and hunches," I told Bill. "They will be correct and will tell you which way to go."

The second few was Ailm.

"The following month you will start to see things more clearly," I said. "It is a sign that you are progressing and moving in the right direction. It also helps your self-esteem and confidence."

The third few was Ruis. Bill already knew the meaning of this one.

"That represents change!" he exclaimed. "That is what I want. But should I do it?"

"Look at the next few," I told him. "That is Beithe, and it represents new beginnings. Four months from now you'll be making a new start. Travel is involved, so you'll be moving to a new location, and good fortune is on your side."

The fifth few was Huathe. "Don't be in too much of a hurry once you move," I said. "This is a sign of restraint. Take your time, make your plans carefully, and allow sufficient time for things to develop. You will need to be patient."

"Not my strong point," Bill agreed.

"Look at the last few—Gort. Keep yourself firmly focused on what you want, and you'll get there. Don't let yourself be sidetracked too much. Listen to the advice of others, but make up your own mind. Don't allow yourself to be influenced by others. If you work toward a specific goal, you will be successful."

Bill was pleased with his reading. He admitted that he had been held back because of the views of others. He talked the matter over with his wife, who turned out to be in favor of the idea after all, and four months later the two of them moved to a charming seaside town. He now works extremely hard all summer long as a Tarot reader, and in the winter months Bill and his wife travel.

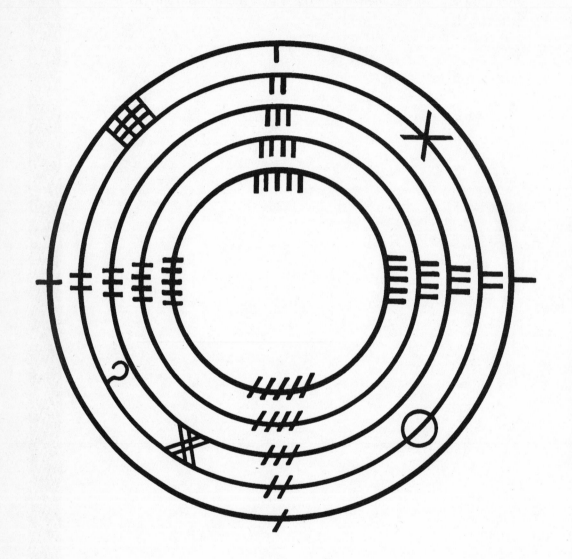

Fionn's Window

CHAPTER THIRTEEN

Fionn's Window

Fionn's window is an ogham meditation mandala named after the legendary Finn (or Fionn) MacCoul. It derives from an attempt to disguise the alphabet so that people who did not know the special arrangement would not be able to read the message. *The Book of Ballymote* records that there were about 150 variants of the ogham script.[1] The origin of Fionn's window is not known, but is believed to date from medieval times.

Fionn's Window depicts each ogham drawn on five differently sized circles, looking rather like an archery target. The first twenty oghams are arranged in the north, south, east, and west positions, with the final five placed midway between them. The exception is between south and west, where two oghams are placed.

In Celtic mythology there were two types of warrior. The more common type was the warrior who lived within a tribe and obeyed the tribal laws. The other was tribeless and obeyed only his own laws. These outlaws formed themselves into groups called Fian or Fenians, which means "battle." These people were the heroes of *The Fenian Cycle*, an enthralling series of stories built up over a period of some 1,500 years.[2]

The Fenians were able to cross easily from one world to another and to take on the shape and characteristics of any animal. They were larger than most men and took part in adventures that were beyond the powers of ordinary people.

Fionn MacCoul was the most famous of all the Fenians. Before Fionn was born, his father, Cumhall, was killed by a man named Goll mac Morna in a savage fight over the leadership of the Fenians. Goll was blinded in one eye in the battle but managed to cut off Cumhall's head and carry it, and all of Cumhall's possessions, away. This marked the start of a feud between the MacCouls and the Mornas.

When Fionn was born, his mother named him Demne and, fearing for his safety, sent him away to be brought up by two women in the center of Ireland. One of these women was a druid and the other a warrior. They taught their secrets to young Fionn, who proved to be an excellent student.

As he grew older, Fionn rebelled against the restrictions placed on him by his foster-parents and ran away. Each time the two women found him and brought him back home.

On one of these adventures, he visited the Plain of Life, where there was a large castle. Boys were playing a game of shinty outside on the grass. Fionn challenged the boys individually to a game and won each one easily. The next day he played against a quarter of the boys and again won easily. The same thing happened the following day when he beat a third of the boys. The boys then challenged him to play them all, and he won again.

The chief inquired about this amazing boy, and the children told him his name was Demne.

"What does he look like?" asked the chief.

"He is tall and fair and very strong," the boys replied.

"In that case, he needs a name more suited to him," the chief declared. "We shall call him Fionn." (Fionn means "fair" in old Irish.)

Fionn's exploits gradually became more widely known, and his foster-mothers told him to leave because they were worried that Goll mac Morna's sons might hear of him and come to kill him.

Fionn entered the service of two kings but was told to move on when they discovered who he was. The sons of Morna had made it known that they were searching for Fionn, and the kings did not want him killed while he was in their service.

Fionn wandered through Ireland engaging in many adventures before meeting an elderly poet called Finneces. Fionn was skilled in soldiery and magic but wanted to become a poet as well, so he decided to stay and study with the old man.

Finneces lived beside a pool on the wide, slow-flowing River Boyne. It was said that the sacred salmon of knowledge lived in this pool, and whoever caught and ate it would gain all the knowledge of the world. Finneces had spent seven years trying to catch the fish. It had been prophesied that a man called Fionn would eat the salmon, and Finneces felt that his name was close enough to fulfill the prediction.

Shortly after Fionn arrived, Finneces managed to catch the salmon and asked Fionn to cook it for him. "Make sure that you do not eat any of it yourself," he said.

He asked again if Fionn had eaten any of it when the fish was served.

"No," Fionn replied. "But I burned my thumb on the hot fish and had to suck it to ease the pain."

"What is your name?" the old poet demanded.

"Demne."

"Do you have any other name?"

"I am called Fionn."

The poet sighed heavily. "Eat the fish, Fionn. It is meant for you."

Fionn ate the salmon of knowledge and gained all the wisdom of the world. From that time on, he could see into the future and know the fate of the world simply by putting his thumb in his mouth.

Shortly after this, Fionn, now wise as well as strong, defeated his enemies and became the king of the Fenians.

There are many stories told about Fionn's adventures. He lived to be more than 230 years old and finally died in battle. However, it is believed that he and his fellow warriors were carried away by people from the Otherworld and are simply sleeping, waiting until the sound of trumpets tells them their beloved Ireland is in danger and needs their help.

Fionn's Window

Fionn's Window, sometimes known as Fionn's Wheel, is a mandala made from the twenty-five ogham letters. It symbolizes wholeness, with the entire universe in balance. The circular structure can be related to Celtic cosmology, the seasons, directions, the Wheel of Life that we will meet in Chapter Sixteen, and even the three circles of being.

Meditating on Fionn's Window can be an enlightening experience. I prefer to meditate on it beside my oracle tree. Sometimes I take the mandala with me and use it as it is. At other times, I take pen and paper with me and draw the mandala while meditating. This is something I learned in India, where it is common for people to draw a yantra in the ground wherever they happen to be. The process of creating the mandala adds enormous power to the meditation process.

The mandala can assist in answering problems in your life. Many times, answers have come to me quite unexpectedly while meditating. In some way, this mandala unlocks and answers problems, creating wholeness in the process.

CHAPTER FOURTEEN

Druid Sticks

We will now move onto another system of divination that also involves small pieces of wood.

Druid sticks are four oblong pieces of wood with a single mark on one side and two marks on the other. When they are cast, or gently thrown, they create one of sixteen possible combinations depending on which side of each stick lands uppermost. The four sticks are then brought together to create a figure that can then be interpreted. They are read from the caster's point of view, with the stick nearest to him or her being the bottom stick of the arrangement.

The origins of druid sticks are not known, but they are obviously reasonably modern. As well as being convenient to carry, the druid sticks are a much simpler, more elegant way of casting the geomantic characters that have been used for divination purposes in many parts of the world for thousands of years.[1] Despite their name, there is no evidence that the ancient druids used geomancy in this form.

Traditionally, they are made from wood because this comes from the earth. Druid sticks are sometimes known as rune sticks. The very name Druid comes from the Celtic *dereu wid*, which means "understanding oak trees." As well as oak, druid sticks were

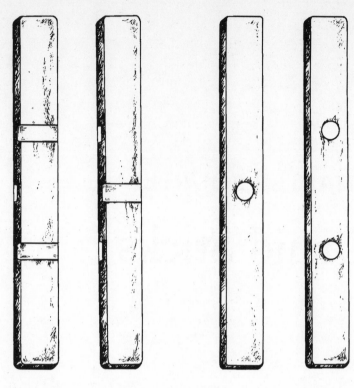

Druid Sticks

traditionally made from the wood of fruit trees. My druid sticks were made by Dusty Cravens of Albuquerque and are of ebony inlaid with holly. However, they can be made from almost any material. At different times, when I have not had my sticks with me, I have used coins, wooden matches, and pieces of cardboard.

You can buy druid sticks from New Age stores, but it is preferable to make your own. They are simple to make. All you need are four oblong sticks about three to six inches long and half to three-quarters of an inch wide. In fact, they can be of any size. A friend of mine, the late Orville Meyer, a well-known Denver psychic, had a miniature set of sticks that were about an inch and a half long, which he carried in his shirt pocket.

On one side of each stick paint a straight line. On the other side paint two straight lines parallel to each other. You may prefer to paint a circle on one side and two circles on the other. Most people start with a very simple set of druid sticks and then make a more attractive set as they become more comfortable with them. As mentioned, in my set the lines are inlaid in holly, and the sticks have been polished. Consequently, they are very attractive and I love using them.

You will also need a casting cloth. Traditionally, the hide of a small animal such as a rabbit was used. I personally prefer to use a piece of dark blue velvet about eighteen inches square.

The four druid sticks are held in one hand and mixed. They are then very gently tossed as the hand moves from the front of the casting cloth to the back. The tossing is virtually a spreading out of the sticks. As soon as all four druid sticks are on the cloth, the right hand rests over them and smooths them out. The tossing and spreading are almost a single movement. By covering them with your hand no one knows what particular combination has been formed until your hand is moved away.

You will have to experiment in casting the druid sticks. The process is very easy, but it takes time to get the knack of allowing the individual sticks to fall away from the hand while also covering the sticks so that they cannot be seen until combined to form a pattern.

It is not necessary to have a set of druid sticks to perform geomancy, but it makes the process much easier. An alternative method is to use a sheet of paper and a pencil. Think about the question you want answered while making a number of rows of dots on the paper. Make the rows of dots from the right hand side of the paper to the left.[2] You will need to make at least sixteen rows of these dots. Once you have done this, count the number of dots in each row. If your total is an odd number, this relates to one dot in the pattern you are forming. An even number of dots create two dots in the pattern. Four rows of dots create a geomantic symbol. For instance:

Row 1 · · · · · · · · · · · · · · · = 15 (odd)   ·
Row 2 · · · · · · · · · · · · · · = 14 (even)   · ·
Row 3 · · · · · · · · · · · · · = 13 (odd)   ·
Row 4 · · · · · · · · · · · · · · = 14 (even)   · ·

This has created the symbol of Amissio—a dot or line at the top with two dots immediately below it, followed by one dot and another two dots.

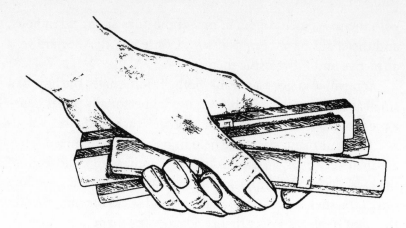

Hold the Sicks in One Hand

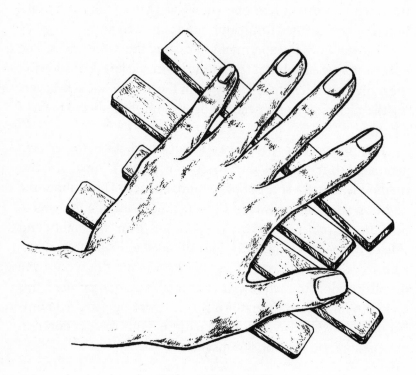

Toss or Spread the Sticks

As you can see, this is a much more laborious way of creating the pictures, but it is practical if you do not have druid sticks with you. This was the method favored by medieval geomancers.

You may prefer to draw a circle on the ground and toss a handful of small stones or coins into it from a few feet away.

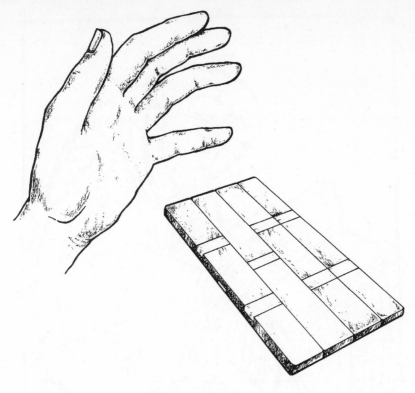

Smooth the Sticks

After each toss count the number of coins inside the circle and create your symbol that way.

Israel Regardie suggested using a bowl full of pebbles.[3] Reach in, take out a handful, and then count them to see if you have an odd or even number. I have a glass bowl full of the stones used for the game of Go, and they make a very attractive display as well as being useful for geomantic purposes.

Israel Regardie also suggested using a pair of dice. After each throw count the numbers on the top of each die to see if they are odd or even.

In Cornwall I met a lady who used a bowl of small gemstones. She would close her eyes and stir the gemstones while thinking about the question. She would then reach in and remove a handful. These were counted in the usual way to see if she had removed an odd or even number. Instead of returning them to the bowl, though, the stones were laid out in a line. They made a particularly beautiful display. Later, while interpreting the

Medieval Geomancer

geomantic symbols she created, she would also interpret the gemstones. She was a gifted healer as well as a psychic reader, and her knowledge of gemstones proved very useful in diagnosis.

Of course, if you want to be really traditional you could make a shallow box at least two feet square and fill it with sand or dry earth. Ensure that this comes from an inland site, because sand from the seashore relates to water. Finally, you need a length of dowel to make rows of dots in the sand. A pencil or any short piece of wood will do, but it is preferable to make a wand for this. This is the method used in Africa, but it does not appear to have been used by the druids.

Anything used for geomantic purposes should be made as beautifully as possible. Do not let anyone else handle your druid sticks, your stones, or even your sandbox. Make sure that you

Geomantic Method Used in Africa

always toss the druid sticks yourself, even when giving a reading for someone else.

Always handle your equipment with respect. You may like to clean the sticks every now and again with salt, or wipe them with oil.

In the next chapter we will cover the basic meanings of each pattern and do a very simple reading.

The Greater Fortune	The Lesser Fortune	Solis ⊙
Via	Populus	Lunae ☽
Aquisitio	Laetitia	Jovis ♃
Puella	Amissio	Veneris ♀
Conjunctio	Albus	Mercurii ☿
Puer	Rubeus	Martis ♂
Carcer	Tristitia	Saturni ♄
☊ Dragon's head	☋ Dragon's taile	

CHAPTER FIFTEEN

The Sixteen Figures

There are sixteen combinations that can be formed by casting the druid sticks. In medieval times the figures were given Latin names that are still being used today, and I have used them here for convenience. Over the years the figures have been related to the seven visible planets, the signs of the Zodiac, the four elements and—rather tenuously—to the tarot.[1]

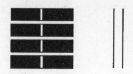

Via—The Way

This combination is formed if all four sticks have one line on them, forming a road or path.[2] This indicates a journey, action, or forward movement. It can also indicate time spent by oneself. Via is related to the moon, water, and the sign of Cancer. The tarot cards most applicable to it are the Chariot and Strength.

As Via is Latin for "street or way," this figure indicates travel. It can also mean the opening of a doorway, such as being exposed to new ideas. Via is an indication that the person has found the right direction and knows where he or she is going. The influence of the moon and Water shows that considerable empathy and understanding is present, and the person has the necessary skill to tactfully get his or her own way. The obstacles that appear from time to time will all be overcome.

Caput Draconis—The Dragon's Head

The Dragon's Head is formed when the top stick shows two lines and the lower three sticks show one line each. This can be construed as the snout of the dragon's head. It traditionally means an entrance or beginning. It is a fortuitous formation because it also indicates shrewdness and alertness.

Caput Draconis relates to Jupiter, earth, the moon's north node, and the sign of Capricorn. The tarot cards are the Star and the Fool.

Caput Draconis is representative of the moon's north node. The nodes indicate the two positions where the moon's path crosses the ecliptic. The north node occurs when the moon ascends from the southern to the northern hemisphere. Caput Draconis is often referred to as the dragon's head, because whenever an eclipse occurs, the dragon moon appears to swallow the sun.

Caput Draconis is a positive figure indicating new starts, birth and innocence. It is an indication of helping others, but remaining aware of one's own needs at the same time. The person has complete faith in what he or she is doing and is "marching to the beat of a different drum."

Puella—The Girl

This formation of the sticks relates to wisdom, intuition, birth, and healing—all traditionally feminine qualities. The sticks show a circle with a line below it, representing the female.

Puella relates to Venus, air, and the sign of Libra. The tarot card is the High Priestess.

Puella means a young girl. It generally relates to pleasant dealings with women and is a good indication of happy family relationships. For a man, it describes his relationship with his wife and daughters. For a woman, it relates to pleasant, harmonious dealings with the other women in her family: mother, mother-in-law, and daughters. It also relates to the traditional feminine qualities of nurturing, wisdom, and intuition. It is not always a positive figure. An attractive woman is not necessarily a good person.

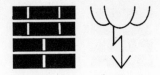

Fortuna Major—Major Fortune

As you can imagine, Fortuna Major means success, friends, harmony, and celebration. It consists of two rows of two lines each, representing the heavens, above two rows of one line each, indicating success coming down from above.

Fortuna Major is related to the sun, fire, and Leo. It relates to the tarot card Justice.

Fortuna Major is a very positive figure indicating great fortune, success, and protection. It relates very much to karma—the good that has been done in the past allows the person to enjoy good luck, success, and peace of mind in the future. It can also relate to property and possessions. It is an indication that the person is liked and held in high esteem by others.

Puer—The Boy

 This formation of the sticks depicts the traditional masculine attributes of physical activity, leadership, initiative, and responsibility. Nowadays, people may not like the idea of masculine and feminine activities being so rigidly defined, but it was a very natural way of deciding things thousands of years ago. The formation of a circle below, with a line above it, represent the male.

Puer relates to Mars, fire, and the sign of Aries. The tarot card is the Magician.

Puer is a positive symbol rather than a negative one, even though it can sometimes indicate rash, impulsive behavior. Traditionally, it was regarded as being positive in war and love but negative in everything else. It usually is indicative of a young man, which could be a son, boyfriend, husband, or bachelor, This person has a great deal of ability, which needs to be harnessed and used correctly. It is an indication to think before acting. Used positively, it is an indication of leadership ability, initiative, and the ability to achieve anything that is desired. All things are possible.

Acquisitio—Gain

This formation of the sticks can be looked at as being two full bowls. It represents prosperity, promotion, improvement, and worldly success.

Acquisitio is related to Jupiter, fire, and the sign of Sagittarius. The tarot card is the Sun.

Acquisitio means "acquiring," particularly in regard to money and possessions. Consequently, this figure relates to success, good fortune, and financial gain. It is a very positive figure. It shows that the trials and travails of the past are now behind the person. He or she has learned from experience and is now on a new cycle of experience. Ideally, this worldly success will give the person the necessary freedom to develop spiritually and intuitively. He or she will enjoy the material rewards and at the same time become aware of philosophy and some of the simple things in life.

Carcer—The Prison

This formation shows the two bowls being held together, confining whatever is inside. It means obstacles, worry, and indecision.

Carcer relates to Saturn, the earth, and Capricorn. The tarot cards are the Devil and the Hanged Man.

Carcer is a negative figure. Because Carcer literally means "a prison," this is a sign of confinement, limitations, and restrictions.

When Carcer appears, the person has to pay particular attention to emotions such as greed, anger, and jealousy. The person has to accept the situation as it is, accept the reversals, and try to remain positive despite periods of doubt and uncertainty.

Tristitia—The Sadness

This time the rune sticks form an upside-down rainbow, indicating disappointment, sorrow, loneliness, and unhappiness.

Tristitia is related to Saturn, air, and the sign of Aquarius. The tarot card is the Tower.

Tristitia means "melancholy" in Latin. It is an indication of grief, sadness, and the possibility of a major loss. These things are likely to happen unexpectedly, and the person will have to cope with the loss or destruction of something that has been carefully built up. The immediate reaction will be to hit out in all directions and blame everyone else. In time, the person will have to learn to be unselfish, charitable, and forgiving.

Cauda Draconis—The Dragon's Tail

The druid sticks form the dragon's tail, meaning the end. It signifies a downward path, an exit, bad luck and ill fortune.

Cauda Draconis relates to the moon's south node, fire, and Scorpio. The tarot cards are Death and Judgment.

Cauda Draconis is a negative figure meaning death, endings, and terminations. Traditionally, it has always been regarded as evil and relates to the negative characteristics of Scorpio.

When Cauda Draconis appears in the chart, the person has to be prepared to walk away from the past and start anew. There will be a great deal of hurt and bitterness, but the person will have to gracefully let go without looking back. He or she will learn a great deal from the experience, and will have to accept that he or she is reaping the rewards of past actions. Cauda Draconis signifies endings, but also portends a new beginning.

Conjunctio—The Union

This formation can be interpreted as a cross, indicating
two people joined together.
It represents love, friendship, partnership, and sexual
attraction.

Conjunctio is related to
Mercury, earth, and the sign
of Virgo. The tarot card is
the Lovers.

Conjunctio is a fortunate
figure indicating a combining, or joining together. Marriage is a
good example of this, though it can also indicate relationships of
all sorts. The person will have to think carefully about what he
or she wants before making any important decisions. These
decisions will have to be made using logic as well as the emotions. The person will have to be responsible and ensure that the
union is beneficial for both parties.

Amissio—The Loss

The druid sticks indicate two upside-down bowls, representing loss, illness, accidents, conflict, and financial difficulties.

Amissio relates to Venus, earth, and the sign of Taurus. The tarot card is the Moon.

Amissio means "loss" and, despite being related to Venus, is a negative figure. It relates to loss, usually of money, but sometimes of love. It indicates a negative outcome to whatever it is the person is involved in. The person will have to be aware of other people's motives and be extremely careful before making decisions. It is a warning to make sure that everything the person does is in everyone's best interest. If he or she tries to take advantage of others, it will assuredly end in failure.

Albeo—The White

The druid sticks picture a full wine glass signifying wisdom, moderation, thoughtfulness, and patience.

Albeo is related to Mercury, air, and Gemini. The tarot cards are Temperance and the Hierophant.

Albeo means contemplation, wisdom, and moderation. It is a fortunate figure, though not as positive as Conjunctio, the other figure governed by Mercury. It can often indicate spiritual growth and the ability to balance all areas of life: physical, mental, and spiritual.

Fortuna Minor—The Minor Fortune

This can be represented as good luck coming from the earth. The figure is formed by two rows of two lines each below two rows of one line each, indicating success coming from the earth. It indicates success, power, possessions, and influence.

Fortuna Minor is, like Fortuna Major, related to the sun, fire, and Leo. However, Fortuna Major is related to the sun during the day, while Fortuna Minor is the sun at night, "placed in lesser dignities." The tarot card represented by it is the Wheel of Fortune.

Fortuna Minor is an indication of lesser success. It shows the person is protected from misfortune and will grow from each experience until success is attained. The person must be prepared to work hard when necessary, but also be willing to slow down, relax, and listen to the quiet voice within from time to time.

Bartholomew of Parma regarded Fortuna Minor as being a negative figure. This is probably because it is ruled by the sun at night, and the person could be inclined to adopt some of the negative qualities of Leo. These would include pride, boastfulness, love of luxury, and the need for constant adulation.

Rubeo—The Red

The druid sticks indicate an upside-down wine glass, representing emptiness. This formation indicates caution and retreat. Because it is red, it is also an indication of passion and temper.

Rubeo is ruled by Mars, water, and the sign of Scorpio. The tarot card is the Hermit.

Rubeo is a negative figure and can indicate passion, negativity, and upheaval, The person needs time for quiet contemplation, to think things through and decide where to go from here. It is a sign of retreat, almost a licking of the wounds, and a gradual awareness that the problems are probably of his or her own making. If the person is prepared to listen to his or her inner self, the correct path for the future will be found.

Laetitia—The Joy

The druid sticks show a rainbow, indicating joy, happiness, good fortune, and peace of mind. This is the most fortunate figure of all.

Laetitia is related to Jupiter, water, and the sign of Pisces. The tarot card is the World.

Laetitia represents joy, laughter, good health, and future happiness. It also relates to creative endeavors and enjoyment of the good things in life. It gives peace of mind, a positive approach to life, and an abundance of happiness and contentment. It usually means that the person has achieved his or her goals, has grown in wisdom, and can now help others. This person has balanced the spiritual and material sides of his or her nature and is living in harmony with the universe.

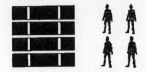

Populus—The People

The druid sticks indicate people standing beside each other.
This figure represents family,
friends, and group involve-
ment.

Populus is also related to
the moon, water, and the sign
of Cancer. The tarot cards are
the   Emperor   and   the
Empress.

Populus literally means
"people" and represents a group or gathering of people. It is a
neutral figure that, like a crowd, tends to reflect its surround-
ings. If love and good, positive thoughts are sent out, the results
will be excellent. However, when negative thoughts and feelings
are sent out the results will work against the person's best interests. The person has to learn from experience, and the future
depends entirely on what use is made of this knowledge. Populus can also mean family, friends, and news or messages.

One Druid Stick Reading

Create all the different combinations with your druid sticks and using your imagination relate them to the pictures suggested. You will learn the basic meanings of each combination very quickly.

Now ask yourself a simple question and cast your rune sticks, or make four rows of marks on a piece of paper. Maybe your question is, "Will my finances improve in the next twelve months?"

Obviously, it will be good news if the rune sticks create Laetitia, Fortuna Major, Fortuna Minor, or Acquisitio.

Equally, the news will not be good if you create Amissio, Cauda Draconis, Tristitia, or Carcer.

What if you create Puella (the girl) or Puer (the boy)? The answer here is not so obvious. With Puella, it could well indicate that financial success comes through using one's intuition. If Puer came up, it would indicate success achieved through hard work and by taking the initiative.

Obviously, Caput Draconis would indicate financial success through a new beginning. This could indicate a change of job, career, or business.

If Conjunctio (the Union) came up, it would indicate financial progress with the aid of someone else—a partnership.

If Rubeo appeared, it would indicate that financial success would occur only if your emotions were kept under control. If you lost your temper at the wrong time, you would seriously damage your chances.

Naturally, this is a quick way of providing an instant answer to a simple question. In the next chapter we will learn how to give a fuller reading.[3]

CHAPTER SIXTEEN

Arthurian Divination

Round about 1150 Geoffrey of Monmouth wrote his verse biography of Merlin, *Vita Merlini*.[1] He had already achieved fame with his earlier work, *History of the Kings of Britain*,[2] written between 1135 and 1139. This book included the life of King Arthur and described Merlin as an adviser to both King Arthur and his father, Uther Pendragon. The *Vita Merlini* carried on the story of Merlin, along with many traditional Celtic ideas, a great deal of cosmology, natural history, classical mythology, and elemental psychology. It also recorded for the first time the Wheel of Life.[3] All of these things had been part of an oral tradition for countless centuries, but Geoffrey of Monmouth was one of the first to write them down.

The Wheel of Life is actually a spiral, and Merlin went around the Wheel many times in the course of the *Vita Merlini*. He underwent nine transformations of consciousness as he gradually grew spiritually.

1. Grief or guilt (North)
2. Compassion (Northeast)
3. Disorientation (East)

4. Sexual liberation (Southeast)
5. Foresight (South)
6. Cosmic vision (Southwest)
7. Curative transformation (West)
8. Liberation from temptation (Northwest)
9. Spiritual enlightenment (North)

At the same time he was experiencing hardship in winter, recalling love in spring, a contest of wills in summer, and learning to benefit from experience in autumn.

Consequently, the Wheel can be interpreted on a number of levels, all of which emphasize growth, development, and ultimate wisdom. It is interesting to consider the saintly Sir Galahad's progress around the Wheel of Life, compared with his father, Sir Lancelot, who was held back spiritually through his adulterous relationship with Guinevere. Interestingly enough, the Grail did not appear in Geoffrey's accounts, being introduced some decades later by Chretien de Troyes in a series of exciting romances. In his account, Sir Galahad achieved virtual spiritual perfection through the Grail.

Arthurian divination is a modern form of numerological geomancy using the Wheel of Life. The nine single digits of numerology cover most facets of human experience. Combined with geomancy, they not only give a vivid picture of the situation and solution, but also show how the outcome will affect other areas of the person's life. For instance, someone may ask a question concerning business. Numerological geomancy will answer this, and at the same time show how the person's family life will be affected, how much work will be involved, whether the outcome will be enjoyable and satisfying, and so on.

After the question has been asked, the druid sticks are cast nine times and the results placed in their respective positions in the Wheel of Life. The result of the first cast will be placed alongside number one, the second cast beside number two, and so on.

It is preferable to ask specific questions, but a good general reading can be obtained by simply asking, "Will the next twelve months be happy for me?" or "What will next year be like?"

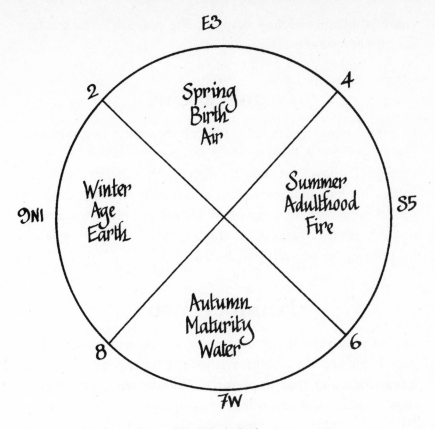

The Wheel of Life

After the sticks have been cast nine times, the results are interpreted. To do this, you have to know the meanings of the nine numbers. As mentioned earlier, it is believed that Pythagoras, the father of modern numerology, learned from the druids and it is fitting that Arthurian geomancy uses the basic meanings of the numbers.[4]

Numerology played a symbolic part in the Celtic myths. We have already seen the significance of number three with the triads. In the myths Amairgen slew the three-headed bird that caused havoc in Ireland. Credné Cred, Goibhniu, and Luchtar were the three gods of craftsmanship.

Five is also significant because there are five great roads in Ireland, five paths of law, and five provinces. Nine was considered a sacred number. It is likely that ancient Celts used a nine-day week. In the myths, Medb rode to Ulster with nine chariots

and Cúchulainn had nine weapons. The curse on Ulster was for nine times nine generations.

Number One

One is the number of the individual. It represents independence and attainment. A good figure in this position bodes well for a successful outcome. A negative figure is an indication of difficulties that have to be overcome. This usually relates to the person asking the question and could relate to ego problems, a rigid outlook, pride, arrogance, or stubbornness. The bards related the number one to unity and purity.

Number Two

Two is the number of tact, diplomacy, and close relationships. A good figure here is a sign that relationships strengthen and grow. It is an indication that the person will be adaptable, good at getting on with others, and willing to compromise when necessary. He or she will be considerate of other people's feelings. It promises quiet success and contentment. A negative figure is an indication that the person will cause problems by being indiscreet or by not paying sufficient attention to his or her partner. The bards related two to "as above, so below."

Number Three

Three is the number of communication, self-expression, and the joys of life. A good figure here is a sign that the person will thoroughly enjoy whatever it is he or she is doing, and will have no difficulties in expressing his or her needs. The person will be optimistic, affectionate, and enthusiastic. The only warning is that the person should not spend too much time on frivolous pursuits. A negative figure is an indication that the person will have a gloomy, dour approach and will make mistakes in expressing him or herself. The bards related the number three to the trinity and the triads.

Number Four

Four is the number of hard work and system and order. A good figure here shows that the person will be prepared to work hard for whatever it is he or she wants. He or she will be well organized and perform the necessary tasks in a logical progression. The bardic description of the number four is "solid," someone who is reliable and can be counted upon. A negative figure here is an indication that the person will be inclined to take shortcuts and compromise the success of the project. He or she will lack motivation and will feel restricted or hemmed in.

Number Five

Five is the number of freedom and variety. It represents change, adventure, and the potential for expansion. A good figure here is an indication that the person will receive many opportunities and will have enough ability to capitalize on them. It can be a sign of success in business. A negative figure here is an indication that the person is at risk of wasting his or her energies and losing the opportunities that are offered. He or she could get lost in overindulgence and end up frustrated, blaming everyone else for his or her misfortune. The bards related number five to the soul and karma. Interestingly enough, five can also be a karmic number in Pythagorean numerology.

Number Six

Six is the number of home and family responsibilities. It represents the domestic side of life. A good figure here shows the person will experience love and support from his or her loved ones. He or she will do everything possible to help and assist them in return. It shows that love sent out will return magnified. A negative figure here is an indication that the person will be unhappy with the home and family. He or she will be resentful when helping others and will feel guilty because of these feelings. In a worst-case scenario, the person could be overwhelmed with

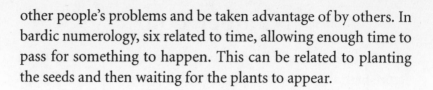

other people's problems and be taken advantage of by others. In bardic numerology, six related to time, allowing enough time to pass for something to happen. This can be related to planting the seeds and then waiting for the plants to appear.

Number Seven

Seven is the number of wisdom and understanding. It relates to spiritual pursuits, intuition, study, and contemplation. A good figure here shows the person will be prepared to listen to his or her inner self and will need time for meditation and contemplation. A negative figure in this position is an indication that the person will pay no attention to the mystical or spiritual side of life and will try and work entirely on the material plane. The bards related seven to the moon and to dreams.

Number Eight

Eight is the number of money and material satisfaction. A good figure here shows that the person will aim high and will ultimately benefit financially from whatever it is he or she is engaged upon. The person will be ambitious, realistic, practical, and down-to-earth in his or her approach. The person will have to work extremely hard and will need to be persistent and remain focused on a specific goal. A negative figure here is an indication that the person will go after his or her dreams of money and financial success in such a way that every other aspect of life will be forgotten. The money, once achieved, will provide little satisfaction. The bards related eight to purification and the yearly cycle.

Number Nine

Nine is the number of humanitarianism, compassion, and giving. Six and nine are both caring numbers. Six gives to loved ones. Nine is more universal and gives to humanity in general. A good figure here shows that the person will be compassionate, understanding, and caring in his or her dealings with others. He or she will give, even when there is no possibility of any return. A negative figure here is an indication that the person will ignore the needs and feelings of others and will put his or her desires first all the time. The bards regarded number nine as containing wisdom and knowledge gained through experience.

The nine numbers can also be placed into groups. For instance, one, four, and eight are all good numbers for business. If the figures in these positions are all favorable, the outcome will be very favorable from a business point of view.

Three, six, and nine are all creative numbers. Good figures in these positions portend well for any form of creativity or self-expression. Interestingly enough, these are good numbers for helping others as well. Six and nine are both humanitarian numbers, and three gives communication skills, which are necessary if one wants to help others effectively.

Now let's ask a question and cast the sticks. For the sake of example, we will ask, "Will John's marriage last?" The sticks are cast nine times and the results recorded. Let's say we ended up with the following:

1 = Via
2 = Fortuna Major
3 = Puella
4 = Amissio
5 = Rubeo
6 = Albeo
7 = Via
8 = Tristitia
9 = Acquisitio

Because the person's question related to marriage, we first look at number two (close relationships), which is Fortuna Major. This is a positive sign, showing not only good luck and success, but also protection.

We now look at number six because that is the number of home and family. Here we have Albeo, the sign of patience and moderation.

It would appear that John's marriage will not only last but will steadily improve. However, patience will be required. Given a reasonable amount of time the marriage will ultimately be a happy and successful one.

We can also look at the other numbers and see how they relate to the question being asked.

Number one is Via. One represents independence. Via is the opening of a door and shows that this independence will be employed in the correct way. It is an indication that John has found the right direction and is being exposed to new ideas.

Number three is Puella. Three relates to self-expression and Puella relates to pleasant dealings with women. John will have few difficulties in expressing himself with the female members of the family. It is a sign of good communication and a happy home life.

Number four is Amissio, the loss. Four relates to hard work and system and order. It appears that John will be impatient and want quick results. He is likely to feel hemmed in or restricted. Too much striving for immediate gain is likely to end up producing the opposite result. John must be prepared to allow matters as much time as necessary to achieve good results.

Number five is Rubeo. Five relates to adventure and freedom. Rubeo is a negative figure connected with the emotions. This is an indication that John must not misuse freedom and should proceed slowly and carefully. He will need to be careful in expressing his emotions and should use his time wisely.

Number seven is Via. We have already come across Via with number one. As we created this chart with nine separate throws of the sticks, it is common to have the same formation appear two or three times. In fact, on one never-to-be-forgotten occasion, I tossed the same figure nine times in a row! Interestingly enough, this created a perfect answer to the question.

Seven relates to wisdom and understanding. Via indicates a door opening. John will have the necessary empathy and understanding to move forward and grow in knowledge and wisdom. There is no limit to how far he could develop in these areas.

Number eight is Tristitia. Eight relates to money and financial matters. Tristitia relates to sadness and disappointment. This is a clear indication that John should not make the pursuit of money his only goal. Success in money matters, assuming it came, would be achieved at too high a cost. On a lesser level it is an indication that he should always look at potential investments very carefully to avoid a loss.

Number nine is Acquisitio, the gain. Nine is the compassionate, humanitarian number. Acquisitio relates to success and good fortune. If John is prepared to help others who are less fortunate, he will reap rich rewards.

Using Arthurian divination, we not only answered the question but also provided a great deal of additional information which helped amplify the answer.

Arthurian divination is particularly useful when someone does not have a specific question and asks something such as, "What does the future hold?", "Will I be happy?", and so on.

You will have noticed that in this particular reading we did not use any of the information in the center of the circle (spring, birth, air, and so on). This information is reserved for questions regarding spiritual growth and development. The Wheel of Life is very useful for answering questions about spiritual growth, because you can follow the development from the earliest stages (winter, earth) through spring, summer, and autumn, ultimately ending up with winter again.

Here is an example. The question is: "Am I moving in the right direction spiritually?" The sticks are cast nine times, producing the following result:

1. Via
2. Caput Draconis
3. Rubeo
4. Puella
5. Acquisitio
6. Fortuna Minor
7. Carcer
8. Tristitia
9. Laetitia

Our imaginary person began his or her spiritual quest in the right way. Number one represents new starts and here we have

Via, indicating forward movement and progress. It will be slow, steady progress, because we are in earth, but it still shows an excellent start.

Number two is still in earth. This is not surprising, because this number indicates patient waiting. At this position we have Caput Draconis, another indication of forward progress. This reveals the start of something significant, which is likely to blossom more in the next stage, which is fueled by air.

With number three we move into air and spring. Air is enthusiastic, stimulated, and interested in everything. Spring is a sign of new life and blossoming. In this position lies Rubeo, a rather unfortunate figure. This indicates that the person will not make the most of this stimulating period, because his or her emotions and temper are likely to get in the way. Fixed ideas will block the potential mental stimulation that is available.

Number four is still in spring, but more staid and rigid in approach. In this position we have Puella. This can indicate a number of things, depending on who our imaginary person is. If it is a man, it could indicate his falling in love. If he is already in a stable relationship, it would indicate a woman who gives him valuable advice concerning spiritual matters. If the person is a woman, this would indicate another woman coming into her life who gives good advice and counsel.

With number five we enter summer. This period is also represented by fire and adulthood. Our imaginary person is no longer as naive as before but still has plenty of energy and drive. In this position we have Acquisitio. This is a sign of good fortune and success. As five relates to variety and freedom, some of the rewards of this success are likely to be spent on travel, which could provide spiritual insight.

Number six is still in summer. The person's thoughts and energies are concerned with home and family matters. This is an indication of positive potential that is presently not being utilized. The person is probably looking far afield for spiritual growth and ignoring the potential at his or her doorstep.

With number seven we move into autumn and maturity. We are now looking at life in a slightly different way, as we have learned and grown from all the experiences that have already taken place. Seven is a spiritual number, making this period an excellent time for inner growth. Unfortunately, though, in this position we have Carcer, indicating constraint and frustration. The person is probably restricted through his or her own outlook and is looking backwards with longing and regret rather than striding into the future.

Number eight is also in autumn. Eight relates to money, and a good figure here denotes relative material comfort in the latter years of life. In this position we have Tristitia, indicating sadness, grief, and the possibility of loneliness. It could even indicate a loss of money in this position. This is not a happy period for our person.

We complete the circle with number nine. We are back in winter again now, and progress is slow and steady. In this position we have Laetitia, the figure of joy, success, and peace of mind. Our anonymous person has recovered from the setbacks of number eight and has achieved his or her goal of spiritual growth. He or she will now also see new potentials and new fields to explore.

Our person's quest is not necessarily over. The Wheel of Life is a spiral, and he or she may have to move around it a number of times to learn the necessary lessons. Remember the different progressions of Sir Lancelot and his son, Sir Galahad? Sir Galahad may have achieved his goal with just one or two progressions. His father never achieved his spiritual goals, no matter how many times he circled the Wheel. The Wheel of Life is a template on which to build and grow.

We can also read the Wheel of Life using the nine transformations given earlier. It can take many lifetimes and numerous circles around the Wheel to work successfully through the nine transformations. There is no need to ask a question when using the transformations, as they are used only for determining spiritual growth.

Here is an example. We have cast the following figures:

1. Puer
2. Albeo
3. Caput Draconis

4. Via
5. Laetitia
6. Cauda Draconis
7. Populus
8. Acquisitio
9. Conjunctio

Our imaginary person starts his or her path with the figure Puer and the transformation of grief or guilt. This would indicate that the person is rash, naive, and impulsive. He or she will be experiencing a sense of grief or guilt because of something he or she did. This stage will be one of gradual maturity. The beardless youth (Puer) slowly grows up.

At the second transformation we have Albeo, which represents wisdom and clear thought. At this stage the subject is learning compassion and will be putting a great deal of mental effort into understanding and learning how to be compassionate.

The third transformation is disorientation. The person will have made much progress in the first two transformations, but will now feel insecure and be unsure where to go from here. The person will be feeling negative and full of conflicting emotions. At this transformation we have Caput Draconis, indicating an entrance, a new start. After a long period of disorientation, our person finally finds a new beginning.

The fourth transformation is sexual liberation. This is a difficult transformation for many people, but our subject is fortunate in having Via at this point. Via indicates the path our subject will travel to liberate him or herself from this transformation.

The fifth transformation is foresight. Our subject is learning to think and plan ahead and also to trust his or her intuition. The figure here is Laetitia, expressing joy, delight, and happiness. As our subject learns from this transformation, he or she will experience enormous satisfaction and pleasure.

The sixth transformation is cosmic vision. Our subject is ideally expanding in awareness and gaining a great understanding of the hidden truths. Unfortunately, in this position we have Cauda Draconis, a negative figure, with its connotations of disaster.

Cauda Draconis indicates a downward journey. Consequently our subject will find it extremely difficult to learn the lesson of this transformation.

In the seventh transformation our subject reaches curative transformation, learning how to heal him or herself and others with the healing power of love. The figure here is Populus, the people, indicating that our subject will have to spread impartial, healing love to a wide range of people. The lesson will not be learned if this transformation is restricted to people who are close to our subject.

The eighth transformation is liberation from temptation. Until this point is reached our subject will be easily tempted by the pleasures of the flesh. At this stage he or she must learn to overcome the attractions of these temptations. The figure here is Acquisitio. It usually relates to gaining money, but can also be interpreted as good fortune and success. It appears that our subject will not experience too many difficulties with this particular transformation.

Finally, we reach the ninth transformation of spiritual enlightenment. Our subject will have thought many times that he or she had reached this point. However, on arriving at the ninth transformation, he or she will realize the amount of work still required to reach ultimate perfection. Our subject has Conjunctio in this position. This signifies a partnership or relationship. In this position it would indicate a partnership with infinite spirit. Once our subject learns to forget the self and become one with God, the goal will be reached.

At the same time as this circle of the Wheel is taking place, our subject will have made many other spirals which are read in the ways discussed earlier.

It is possible to reach perfection in just one turn around the Wheel. It is more usual for the subject to make several revolutions, and these could be spread over many lifetimes. It is also possible for a subject to remain fixed in one position, unable to progress further in this lifetime. Sir Lancelot is a good example of this, as he would likely have become fixed at transformation four. Even if he progressed again, transformation eight would have held him back.

As you can see, the Wheel of Life can be used in a number of different ways, all of which are extremely valuable. It can be used simply for a general reading. It can also be used to measure spiritual progress and to give indications of where to go from here. Finally, through the nine transformations, we can see how we slowly evolve over a lifetime or lifetimes.

CHAPTER SEVENTEEN

Other Forms of Celtic Divination

In this book I've tried to include the forms of Celtic divination that are most practical today. In fact, the Celts had a wide range of methods for divination. Many of these were used only at particular times of the year. An example is the Halloween rite, where girls scattered linseed or hemp seed while calling on their future husbands to come and collect it. The phantom form of the husband then appeared.

At Winter's Eve in Wales it was believed that if you stood on a church porch until midnight you would hear a voice calling out the names of the people who were going to die in the following year. Of course, you ran the risk that you might hear your own name.

The Greek and Roman historians were fascinated with the druids mainly because of their practices of human sacrifice and headhunting. They tended to ignore that, not much earlier in their own histories, they had been indulging in similar types of activity. It is likely these writers deliberately emphasized this aspect of Celtic divination to demonstrate how primitive and barbaric the druids were.

The main purpose of human sacrifice was divination. Both Diodorus Siculus and Strabo described the druidic custom of

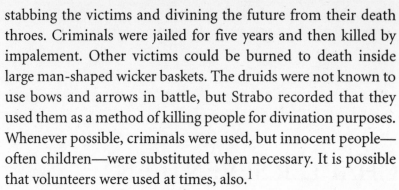

stabbing the victims and divining the future from their death throes. Criminals were jailed for five years and then killed by impalement. Other victims could be burned to death inside large man-shaped wicker baskets. The druids were not known to use bows and arrows in battle, but Strabo recorded that they used them as a method of killing people for divination purposes. Whenever possible, criminals were used, but innocent people—often children—were substituted when necessary. It is possible that volunteers were used at times, also.[1]

Julius Caesar interpreted this to mean that the druidic gods could be appeased only by sacrificing one human life for another. Pomponius Mela wrote in the first century A.D. that the Celts had ceased sacrificing humans. He did not say if this was because of Roman influence.

Fortunately, most other methods of druidic divination did not involve a human sacrifice. Because the Celts were so attuned to nature, many methods of divination revolved around the movements of birds and other animals. The flight of certain birds, particularly wrens, ravens, and cranes, could be interpreted. The wren was known as "the devil's bird" in some parts of England because its song was interpreted by the druids.

Magpies were regarded with great superstition. Seeing one magpie was considered one of the worst omens, but fortunately things improved when two or more magpies were found together. An old English rhyme tells the story:

> One for sorrow
> Two for mirth.
> Three for a wedding
> Four for a birth.
> Five for rich
> Six for poor,
> Seven for a witch,
> I can tell you no more.

A number of things could be done to avert the disaster that was bound to follow after seeing a single magpie. One could greet the bird kindly by raising a hand or curtsying.

Alternatively, one could make a sign of the cross on one's chest, or cross the thumbs.[2]

Other animals were frequently used as well. Boudicca released a hare and watched it run for intimations on how best to fight the Romans. Diodorus wrote: "These men (druids) predict the future by observing the flight and calls of birds, and by the sacrifice of holy animals: all orders of society are in their power."

Fires were sometimes lit for the purpose of divination. The shape and direction of the smoke was then interpreted. Seers could also see pictures in the golden-red flames of a peat fire. This was known as fire-gazing. Divination by tossing stones into a fire has already been mentioned.

Dreams were of great importance. To determine the identity of a future king, a special procedure was followed known as *tarbfeis,* "bull-feast." A bull was ritually killed and the seer ate the flesh and drank some blood. He would then go to sleep wrapped in the bull's hide and would hopefully capture the king's name while dreaming.

A similar procedure, known as *taghairm,* used the hide of an ox. Spirits came to the aid of the seer to help produce the required prophetic dreams.

Imbas-forosnai was a trance caused by eating the flesh of a white bull at the time of the winter solstice. After incarnations had been said over the diviner's hands, he would go to sleep with his right hand covering his left eye and his left hand covering the right eye. Chants would be said while the seer slept, and again his dreams would provide prophecies.

The entire ancient world practiced animal sacrifice. It was a natural thing to do, because it incorporated both the offering up of wealth and also a death, which is the ultimate sacrifice.

If a woman dreamed of any fruit that was out of season, it was regarded as a sign of conception. Any fears a mother had were believed to be passed on to her children.

Scapulimancy was divination from shoulder blades. The shoulder blade was cleaned and the surface divided into several areas that were then interpreted. It is interesting to note that the ancient Chinese used a similar method of divination.

The Celts also practiced oracular incubation. Nicander of Colophon recorded that they would spend the night beside the ashes of a dead person and see what predictions would come to them. No other race of people is known to have done this. The Greeks used the same system for a different purpose. Rather than for divination, they would place their sick people beside the ashes in the hope that they would be healed by their god Asklepios.

Divination from the flight patterns of birds (ornithomancy) has already been mentioned. The Etruscans and Romans used a similar system, but we do not know if the Celts used it after certain weather patterns as the Romans did.

An old tale tells the story of Mog Ruith, a West Munster druid who was able to fly over the heads of an opposing army, while wearing a bird costume, and bring back details of the enemy.[2] This is obviously an account of astral travel.

Channeling is far from being a new phenomenon, and instances have been recorded dating back three thousand years. Bards known as *awenyddion* were regularly consulted by people wanting to know the future. The diviners would become entranced and start answering questions. Gerald of Wales, writing in the twelfth century when awenyydion were still to be found, concluded that the diviners were taken over by spirits or demons.

The druids practiced astrology, and buildings were erected at the times astrologers deemed to be most propitious. The Irish term for astrologer was *néladoir,* which means "cloud-diviner." In the Irish myths, Cathbad the druid cast Deirdre's horoscope when she was born. He prophesied that she would be the fairest woman in all of Ireland and would marry a king, but because of her ruin and death would come to the land.

Last century the remains of an enormous bronze plaque were found near Bourg-en-Bresse in France, which proves how knowledgeable the Celts were about astronomy. This Coligny Calendar, as it has been named, is a lunar-solar calendar that reconciles the two cycles. The bronze is engraved with sixty-two consecutive lunar months and two intercalary months. It was made around 50 B.C. and is one of the oldest inscriptions in a Celtic language to be found so far. Although Roman numbers and letters are used, the words and the arrangement of the calendar are Celtic.

Julius Caesar wrote that the druids enjoyed long discussions about the movements of the heavenly bodies. Cicero also recorded that the druids' knowledge of astrology was comparable with the Greeks. The triad called "The three renowned astronomers of the Island of Britain" listed Idris the giant, Gwydion ap Don, and Gwynn ap Nudd, and finished with, "Such was their knowledge of the stars, their natures and qualities, that they were able to predict whatsoever they desired until the Day of Doom."

John Dee, the celebrated astrologer of Elizabethan England, was Welsh, so was likely to have used ideas from Celtic astrology in his readings. In this system of astrology, it was believed that people born at night were able to see ghosts and were open to visions. Children born during a storm were destined to lead difficult lives.

The druids at the time of Arthur studied the influences of the planets on the four elements of fire, earth, air, and water to attain a pure soul. From this came the sense of chivalry that was so much a part of the life of King Arthur's knights.[4]

The famous Welsh poem, *Spoils of Annwn,* attributed to Taliesin, was written down in the sixth century but is probably much older than that. It outlines a series of adventures undertaken by King Arthur and twelve knights. They sailed on his boat, *Prydwen,* to Annwn, the Other World, to bring back a magic cauldron. The entire poem symbolizes the twelve signs of the Zodiac, plus King Arthur, the thirteenth, representing the sun.[5] Christine Hartley suggests that the name Arthur comes from Airem, a sun god of Irish myth. So Arthur was the sun god, the king who corresponds to Jupiter in Celtic mythology. His sign of the zodiac was Aries.[6]

Both men and women practiced divination. Women diviners were usually either druidesses or related to druids. They were called *allrune,* which means "all knowing."

CHAPTER EIGHTEEN

Conclusion

The golden age of Celticism is far from over. Celtic music is being listened to by more people than ever before. Celtic art is enjoying a renaissance. Celtic jewelry holds a mysterious fascination for many. The Celtic myths are now being talked about in the same breath as the ancient Greek and Roman myths.

Because the druids were so intent on keeping their secrets, much of their teaching has been lost. Fortunately, enough remains for us to build up a realistic picture of life in Celtic Europe. We have gone beyond the idealistic romanticism that surrounded the Celts last century. True, it is still easy to conjure up pictures of white-robed druids performing strange rituals in groves of oak trees, but archaeologists have produced evidence of some of the less desirable aspects of the druidic religion to provide a balance.

The Greek and Roman writers assumed that the Celts were uncivilized and much of their work was designed to promote belief in that hypothesis. Fortunately, enough remains for us to realize how cultured and advanced the Celts really were. We can still learn a great deal today from their theology, medicine, education, music, and art.

It is my belief that many forms of druid divination are just as useful today as at any other time. I have proved it to my own satisfaction many times. Now it is up to you. Find some stones. Make yourself a bodhran drum or some oghams or druid sticks. You will find that with them you can tap into the Celtic psyche and receive insights that you would not otherwise have discovered.

Notes

Titles are given with details of the publisher and date of publication on the first mention only.

Chapter One

1. Peter Berresford Ellis, *A Dictionary of Irish Mythology* (London: Constable and Company, 1987), 5.

2. Tim Newark, *Celtic Warriors 400 BC–1600 AD* (Poole: Blandford Press, 1986), 15–7.

3. T.G.E. Powell, *The Celts* (Rev. ed. London: Thames and Hudson, 1980), 13-4.

4. Julius Caesar, *The Gallic War and Other Writings.* (New York: Random House, Inc., 1957; London: Heron Books, 1969), 11–3.

5. Caesar, *Gallic War.* Bk. 6, ch. 13 and 14.

6. Editors of Time-Life Books, *A Soaring Spirit 600–400 BC. Time-Life History of the World Series* (Amsterdam: Time-Life Books, 1988), 111.

7. Peter Berresford Ellis, *Caesar's Invasion of Britain* (London: Orbis Publishing, 1978), 62–3.

8. Time-Life, *A Soaring Spirit*, 114.

9. Frank Delaney, *The Celts* (1986), 32.

10. Powell, *The Celts*, 171; Peter Harbison, *Pre-Christian Ireland* (London: Thames and Hudson, 1988), 152-153; Charles Thomas, *Celtic Britain* (London: Thames and Hudson, 1986). On page 31 is a photograph of a 1976 reconstruction of a circular farmhouse.

11. Delaney, *The Celts*, 32.

12. Ellis, *Caesar's Invasion of Britain*, 26–7.

13. Ibid., 63.

14. Ibid., 66–7.

15. Marc Alexander, *British Folklore, Myths and Legends* (London: Weidenfeld and Nicolson, 1982), 153–8.

Chapter Two

1. Alexander, *British Folklore*, 31–2.

2. Ibid., 52.

3. Morris Marples, *White Horses and Other Hill Figures* (1949. Reprint. Gloucestershire: Alan Sutton Publishing Limited, 1981), 53. This interesting book discusses the origin of the seventeen chalk horses. Some authorities claim the Uffington White Horse was built to celebrate an historic event, others that it was a landmark to show travelers that they were going in the right direction.

4. Don Robins, *The Secret Language of Stone* (London: Rider, 1988), 38.

5. The training of a bard varied slightly in England, Ireland and Wales. Philip Carr-Gomm writes that the training lasted twelve years in Ireland and at the end of that time the bard knew 350 different stories. He gives an excellent description

of each year of training in his excellent book, *The Elements of the Druid Tradition* (Dorset: Element Books, 1991), 44.

6. William Blake, the eighteenth-century visionary poet and mystic, wrote *Songs of Experience* in 1794. The dark, often gloomy poems in this book contrast sharply with his earlier book, *Songs of Innocence* (1789), which has divine love and understanding as its theme. Together, these two books deal with "the two contrary states of the human soul."

7. Eleanor Merry, in her book *The Flaming Door* (London: Rider and Company, 1936), tells the esoteric story of the druids in Atlantis. She describes a war between the powers of black and white magic. In the final eruption that engulfed Atlantis, the white sages were the only ones who survived, and they headed to Ireland, England, and America in small boats. Consequently, both the Druid and the native American traditions date back to the days of Atlantis. Christine Hartley gives more information on this subject in *The Western Mystery Tradition* (Wellingborough: The Aquarian Press, 1986), 22–6.

8. William Klingaman, *The First Century* (Harper Collins, 1990; London: Hamish Hamilton Limited, 1991), 284–5.

9. R. J. Stewart, *Celtic Gods, Celtic Goddesses* (London: Blandford, 1990), 104.

10. Hartley, *Western Mystery Tradition*, 92.

11. Ibid., 96–7.

12. Ibid., 99.

13. Anthony Birley, *Life in Roman Britain* (Rev. ed. London: B. T. Batsford Ltd, 1981), 137.

14. *The New Encyclopedia Britannica* (15th ed. Chicago: Encyclopedia Britannica, Inc., 1983), *Micropedia* 1:812.

15. Dai Smith, *Wales! Wales?* (London: George Allen and Unwin, 1984), 34.

16. The Order of Bards, Ovates and Druids was established in 1964 and runs correspondence courses, workshops, and

retreats. Information on their programs can be obtained from: The Order of Bards, Ovates and Druids, 260 Kew Road, Richmond, Surrey, TW9 3EG, England.

17. Ross Nichols, *The Book of Druidry* (London: The Aquarian Press, 1990), 114–8.

18. R. Bromwich, *Trioedd Ynys Prydein: The Welsh Triads* (2d ed. Cardiff: University of Wales Press, 1978).

19. Ellis, *Dictionary of Irish Mythology,* 223,

20. Nichols, *Book of Druidry,* 273.

21. Eleanor C. Merry, *The Flaming Door* (London: Rider and Company, London, 1936. Rev. and enlarged ed. East Grinstead: New Knowledge Books, 1963; Edinburgh: Floris Books, 1983), 126.

22. Edward Williams, *Bardass* (Llandovery: Llandovery Society for Preservation of Welsh Manuscripts, n.d.).

23. R. Brasch, *The Book of the Year* (North Ryde, Australia: Angus and Robertson, 1991), 5, 6.

24. Stewart, *Celtic Gods, Celtic Goddesses,* 38–9.

25. Zolar, *Zolar's Encyclopedia of Omens, Signs and Superstitions* (New York: Prentice Hall Press, 1989), 356–7.

26. There are a number of translations of Amairgen's poem. This version is from *The Irish Mythological Cycle* by H. D'Arbois de Jubainville, published in Ireland in 1903. It is a translation of his *L'Epopée Celtique en Ireland* (Paris, 1884). It can also be found in T.W. Rolleston's *Myths and Legends of the Celtic Race* (London: Harrap and Company, 1911; London: Constable and Company, 1985). A very similar translation to that of de Jubainville may be found in Ellis's *Dictionary of Irish Mythology,* page 30. The R.A.S. Macalister translation can be found in Alwyn and Brinley Rees's *Celtic Heritage,* page 98. R.J. Stewart provides yet another version in his excellent work, *Celtic Gods, Celtic Goddesses,* page 134. Robert Graves rearranged the poem and provided an extensive commentary in *The White Goddess.*

Chapter Three

1. Alexander, *British Folklore*, 11.

2. Anne Ross, *Druids, Gods and Heroes from Celtic Mythology* (London: Peter Lowe, 1986), 102. Anne Ross and Don Robins, *The Life and Death of a Druid Prince* (London: Rider and Company, 1989), 152–3. The Coligny Calendar is preserved in the Palais des Arts, Lyons, France.

3. Ellis, *Caesar's Invasion of Britain*, 32.

4. Powell, *The Celts*, 144.

5. Ronald Hutton, *The Pagan Religions of the Ancient British Isles* (Oxford: Blackwell Publishers, 1991), 177.

6. Hartley, *Western Mystery Tradition*, 71, 106.

7. Alexander, *British Folklore*, 11.

8. Powell, *The Celts*, 148.

9. Ellis, *Caesar's Invasion of Britain*, 34. Janet and Stewart Farrar devote an entire chapter to Brighid in *The Witches' Goddess* (London: Robert Hale Limited, 1987), 96–103. They also discuss the human St. Bridget who died about 525 A.D.

10. Brasch, *Book of the Year*, 61.

11. Powell, *The Celts*, 148.

12. W.R. Wilde, *Irish Popular Superstitions* (1852. Reprint. Dublin: Irish Academic Press Limited, 1979), 42.

13. Ellis, *Dictionary of Irish Mythology*, 41.

14. Lugh is the Irish name for this god who was also known as Lud in England, Lleu in Wales, and Lugus in Gaul. London and Lyons in France are both named after him.

15. Powell, *The Celts*, 149.

16. Philip Carr-Gomm, *The Elements of the Druid Tradition* (Dorset: Element Books Limited, 1991), 73.

Chapter Four

1. The symbolism of this poem is discussed in Hartley, *Western Mystery Tradition*, 61–2.

2. J. Gwenogvryn Evans, ed., *The Black Book of Caemarthen* (Pwllheli, 1906); Norma Lorre Goodrich, *Merlin* (New York: Franklin Watts, 1987), 289. Goodrich reports the research of H.L.D. Ward, who studied the Welsh poetry attributed to Merlin. His conclusions were that the poems had been so rewritten in the twelfth century that they were valueless, both as documents and as poetry. *The Black Book of Caemarthen,* one of the four ancient books of Wales, was written in the reign of Henry II and consists of fragments of texts that have failed to survive in complete form. Examples are sections from an early version of Tristan and Iseult and a history of Myrddin Wyllt, explaining how he went mad at the sight of battle and had the gift of prophecy. *The Black Book of Caermarthen* also contains some of the earliest Welsh religious poetry. Professor Gwynn Williams, in *An Introduction to Welsh Literature* (Cardiff: University of Wales Press, 1978), thinks that some of Merlin's poems date from the sixth century, but others are pastiches dating from twelfth or thirteenth centuries (page 5). The original manuscript is in the National Library of Wales in Aberystwyth. Like many other medieval Welsh manuscripts, the *Black Book of Caermarthen* was named from the color of its binding.

3. Geoffrey of Monmouth, *History of the Kings of Britain* (Trans. with an introduction by Lewis Thorpe. London: Penguin Books, 1966), 144–62.

4. Gwyn Jones and Thomas Jones, trans., *The Mabinogion* (London: J. M. Dent and Sons, 1949), 89–94.

5. Douglas Monroe, *The 21 Lessons of Merlyn* (St. Paul: Llewellyn Publications, 1992). This book is really two works in one. One is a brilliant historical novel about the first fifteen years of Arthur's life. The second is a comprehensive text on druid magic.

6. Graham Phillips and Martin Keatman, *King Arthur: The True Story* (London: Century, 1992), 35.

7. Goodrich, *Merlin,* 123–57. Goodrich includes a superb translation of Merlin's prophecies.

8. There have been a number of versions of the Thirteen Treasures of Britain. Here are the items usually listed:

- The sword Dyrnwyn of Rhydderch Hael. This sword would burst into flame if anyone, apart from its rightful owner, drew it from its scabbard.

- The Basket of Gwyddno Garenhir. This basket increased food that was placed into it a hundred times.

- The Horn of Bran Galed. This horn could produce any drink that was desired.

- The Chariot of Morgan Mwynvawr. This chariot would instantly transport anyone who sat in it to wherever they wished to go.

- The Halter of Clydno Eiddyn. Any horse that was desired would immediately appear in the halter.

- The Knife of Llawfrodded Farchawg. This knife could serve meat to twenty-four men at the same time.

- The Cauldron of Tyrnog. This cauldron would instantly cook food for a brave person, but would not produce any for a coward.

- The Whetstone of Tudwal Tudclud. The whetstone would sharpen the swords of brave men but do nothing for the swords of cowards.

- The Garment of Padarn Beisrudd. This would look superb on a man of gentle birth, but would not fit other people.

- The Pan of Rhegynydd Ysgolhaig. The pan and platter (below) would instantly produce whatever food was desired.

- The Platter of Rhegynydd Ysgolhaig.

- The Golden Chessboard of Gwenddolen. This chessboard contained chesspieces made of silver, which were able to play all by themselves when placed on the board.

• The Mantle of Arthur. This mantle granted invisibility. Anyone who wore it was able to see everything but be invisible to others.

Chapter Five

1. Ellis, *Dictionary of Irish Mythology,* 212.

2. Robins, *Secret Language of Stones,* 32.

3. Jack Whyte, *The Skystone* (Toronto: Penguin Books Canada Limited, 1992).

4. Monroe, *21 Lessons of Merlyn,* 374–6.

5. *The New Encyclopedia Britannica. Micropedia* 3:599.

6. Homer, *The Iliad* (16.234) and *The Odyssey* (14.327). There are many translations available. The versions I like most are the translations by Robert Fitzgerald (New York: Doubleday, 1975). Homer's mention that the priests did not wash their feet and slept on the ground is an indication that the sanctuary was extremely old. Washing of feet and sleeping in beds was comparatively modern in Homer's day.

7. Georg Luck, *Arcana Mundi* (Baltimore: John Hopkins University Press, 1985), 264. Luck also lists a number of the questions that were asked at Dodona. The questions were written on thin lead tablets and were stored in the sanctuary archives. A man asked if his wife would become pregnant. He had remained childless in his earlier marriage and was becoming impatient with his second wife. Another man asked if he was the father of the child his wife was carrying. A man called Cleotas asked if it would be profitable for him to keep cattle. A lady called Nicocrateia asked which god she should make a sacrifice to in order to become well again. A wealthy man called Timotheus asked if it would be appropriate for him to build a temple of Aphrodite and allow it to be public property. The reply was positive, providing Timotheus had the decree, the oracle, and the request inscribed on a stone slab in the temple (pages 265–6).

8. Nigel Pennick, *Games of the Gods* (London: Rider and Company, 1989, 26; *Secret Games of the Gods*, New York: Samuel Weiser, Inc., 1992).

9. Monroe, *21 Lessons of Merlyn*, 275.

10. Max Maven, *Max Maven's Book of Fortunetelling* (New York: Prentice Hall, 1992), 62.

11. Hutton, *Pagan Religions of the Ancient British Isles*, 294.

Chapter Six

1. James Bonwick, *Irish Druids and the Old Irish Religions* (1894. Reprint. New York: Dorset Press, 1986), 313–20.

2. Ibid., 57.

3. Alexander, *British Folklore*, 43.

4. Ibid., 44. The author also tells how colored pebbles were at one time used as a protection against drowning.

5. Eric Maple, *Old Wive's Tales* (London: Robert Hale, 1981), 34. In this book, Maple writes that the Brahan Seer was killed by being thrown into a barrel of burning tar. Elizabeth Sutherland has made extensive research into the life and prophecies of the Brahan Seer. Her *Ravens and Black Rain* (London: Constable and Company, 1985) outlines his story and includes many of his prophecies. She has also written a novel based on his life, *The Seer of Kintail* (London: Constable, 1974), and edited *The Prophecies of the Brahan Seer* by Alexander Mackenzie (London: Constable, 1977).

Chapter Seven

1. Kaledon Naddair, *Keltic Folk and Faerie Tales* (London: Century Hutchinson Ltd, 1987), 40. This remarkable book delves deeply into Celtic shamanistic lore, and the symbolism of minerals, plants, animals, and faeries.

2. Carr-Gomm, *Elements of the Druid Tradition*, 48–9.

3. Brasch, *Book of the Year*, 34.

Chapter Eight

1. T. Gwynn Jones, *Welsh Folklore and Folk-Custom* (1930. Reprint. Cambridge: D.S. Brewer, 1979; Totowa, NJ: Rowman and Littlefield, 1979), 169.

Chapter Nine

1. Hans Jensen, *Sign, Symbol and Script* (London: George Allen and Unwin, 1970), 579. This book is a translation of the third, revised edition of *Die Schrift in Vergangenheit und Gegenwort*, first published in Germany in 1935.

2. *The Book of Ballymote* is a fourteenth-century Irish manuscript, parts of which are believed to have been copied from ninth-century texts. It can be found in the library of the Royal Irish Academy in Dublin. This manuscript is the main source of information about ogham, and includes an account of why Ogma invented it: "Ogma, being a man much skilled in dialects and poetry, invented Ogham, its object being for signs of secret speech known only to the learned, and designed to be kept from the vulgar and poor of the nation."

3. Jensen, *Sign, Symbol and Script*, 579–80.

4. Ellis, *Dictionary of Irish Mythology*, 187.

Chapter Ten

1. Neil Ewart, *The Lore of Flowers* (Dorset: Blandford Press, 1982), 61–2.

Chapter Twelve

1. This is my own version of laying out the oghams, and one that I have found particularly useful. Other versions can be found in *The Celtic Tree Oracle, The Book of Ogham,* and *The Celtic Oracle* (see Suggested Reading, page 195).

Chapter Thirteen

1. Nigel Pennick, *The Secret Lore of Runes and Other Ancient Alphabets* (London: Rider, 1991), 152.

2. Douglas Hyde, *A Literary History of Ireland* (T. Fisher Unwin, 1899; London: Ernest Benn Limited, 1967; New York: Barnes and Noble, Inc., 1967), 363–86.

Chapter Fourteen

1. Information on the history of geomancy can be found in *The Oracle of Geomancy* by Stephen Skinner (Dorset and San Leandro: Prism Press, 1977). The Yoruba system of geomancy still used today in West Africa is described in *A Recitation of Ifa, Oracle of the Yoruba* by Judith Gleason (New York: Grossman Publishers, 1973). The medieval system of astrological geomancy is described in *The Complete Book of Astrological Geomancy* by Priscilla Schwei and Ralph Pestka (St. Paul: Llewellyn Publications, 1990).

2. Cornelius Agrippa (attrib.), *Fourth Book of Occult Philosophy* (London: Askin Publishers, 1978), 5.

3. Israel Regardie, *Practical Guide to Geomantic Divination* (London: Aquarian Press, 1972), 8.

Chapter Fifteen

1. Dusty Cravens, *Runic Geomancy* (Albuquerque: Flora and Company, 1989).

2. The idea of using the picture created by the pattern of druid sticks is a modern one which was developed as a mnemonic device. It was first shown to me many years ago by Dusty Cravens and later appeared in his *Runic Geomancy*. A similar system can also be found in *Max Maven's Book of Fortunetelling* (New York: Prentice Hall, 1992), 65–7.

3. Instructions on how to give a geomantic reading as done in the time of Cornelius Agrippa can be found in *The Oracle of Geomancy* by Stephen Skinner (Prism Press, 1977), 39–50.

Chapter Sixteen

1. Geoffrey of Monmouth, *Vita Merlini*. A translation by B. Clarke was published by the University of Wales, Cardiff, in 1973. Not everyone believes that Geoffrey of Monmouth wrote the *Vita Merlini*. Norma Lorre Goodrich, in her book *Merlin*, page 96, ridicules the suggestion, describing the author as being a "comical poet."

2. Geoffrey of Monmouth, *The History of the Kings of Britain*. The translation by Lewis Thorpe was published by Penguin Books Ltd., London, in 1966.

3. A detailed description of the Wheel of Life can be found in an article by R.J. Stewart called "Merlin, King Bladud, and the Wheel of Life," published in *The Book of Merlin* (ed. R.J. Stewart. London: Blandford Press, 1988), 111–46.

4. Alexander Thom, *Megalithic Sites in Britain* (Oxford: Oxford University Press, 1967). Astro-archaeology is providing further proof that the ancient Britons used a system of mathematics that is virtually the same as the one we call Pythagorean. Professor Thom surveyed several hundred stone circles and megaliths all over Britain and concluded that they were all designed to a uniform standard, similar to Pythagorean geometry. But they were built more than a thousand years before Pythagoras was born!

Chapter Seventeen

1. Robins, *The Life and Death of a Druid Prince.* In this book, the authors put forward a convincing argument that their prince volunteered to become a sacrifice.

2. Don Lewis, *Religious Superstition Through the Ages* (London: A. R. Mowbray and Company, 1975), 100.

3. Caitlin and John Matthews, *The Western Way* (London: Arkana Paperbacks, 1985), 33.

4. Merry, *The Flaming Door,* 113. This book provides an excellent introduction to the mysteries.

5. Ibid., 109–13.

6. Hartley, *Western Mystery Tradition,* 45–6.

Suggested Reading

Ashe, Geoffrey. *Mythology of the British Isles*. London: Methuen, 1990.

Bonwick, James. *Irish Druids and the Old Religions*. New York: Dorset, 1986.

Brunaux, Jean Louis. *The Celtic Gauls: Gods, Rites and Sanctuaries*. Trans. Daphne Nash. London: B.A. Seaby, 1987.

Caesar, Julius. *The Conquest of Gaul*. Trans. S. A. Handford. London: Penguin Books, 1951.

Carr-Gomm, Philip. *The Elements of the Druid Tradition*. Dorset: Element Books, 1991.

Delaney, Frank. *The Celts*. London: BBC Publications, 1986

Gantz, Jeffrey (trans.). *The Mabinogion*. London: Penguin Books, 1976.

Graves, Robert. *The White Goddess*. London: Faber & Faber, 1952.

Green, Miranda. *The Gods of the Celts*. Gloucester: Alan Sutton, 1986.

Hartley, Christine. *The Western Mystery Tradition.* Wellingborough: The Aquarian Press, 1968.

Jones, T. Gwynn. *Welsh Folklore and Folk-Custom.* 1930. Reprint. Cambridge: D.S. Brewer, 1979.

Laing, Lloyd. *Celtic Britain.* London: Routledge and Kegan Paul, 1979.

Larrington, Carolyne, ed. *The Feminist Companion to Mythology.* London: Pandora Press, 1992.

MacCana, Proinsias. *Celtic Mythology.* London: Newnes Books, 1983.

Mallory, J.P. *In Search of the Indo-Europeans.* London: Thames and Hudson, 1989.

Matthews, Caitlin. *Elements of Celtic Tradition.* Dorset: Element Books, 1989.

Matthews, Caitlin and John. *The Western Way: A Practical Guide to the Western Mystery Tradition.* Vol. 1. London: Arkana Paperbacks, 1985.

Matthews, John. *Elements of Arthurian Tradition.* Dorset: Element Books, 1989.

Maven, Max. *Max Maven's Book of Fortunetelling.* New York: Prentice Hall, 1992.

Merry, Eleanor. *The Flaming Door.* London: Rider and Company, 1936.

Michell, John. *The Earth Spirit: Its Ways, Shrines and Mysteries.* London: Thames and Hudson, 1975.

Monroe, Douglas. *The 21 Lessons of Merlyn.* St. Paul: Llewellyn Publications, 1993.

Murray, Liz and Colin. *The Celtic Tree Oracle.* New York: St. Martin's Press, 1988.

Nichols, Ross. *The Book of Druidry.* London: Aquarian Press, 1990.

Pennick, Nigel. *The Secret Lore of Runes and other Ancient Alphabets.* London: Rider and Company, 1991.

Pennick, Nigel, and Nigel Jackson. *The Celtic Oracle.* London: Aquarian Press, 1992.

Phillips, Graham, and Martin Keatman. *King Arthur: The True Story.* London: Century, 1992.

Powell, T.G.E. *The Celts.* London: Thames and Hudson, 1980.

Rees, Alwyn, and Brinley Rees. *Celtic Heritage.* London: Thames & Hudson, 1961.

Rolleston, T.W. *Myths and Legends of the Celtic Race.* London: George G. Harrap & Company, 1911.

Ross, Anne. *Pagan Celtic Britain.* London: Routledge and Kegan Paul, 1967.

Ross, Anne. *The Pagan Celts.* London: Routledge and Kegan Paul, 1986.

Ross, Anne, and Don Robins. *The Life and Death of a Druid Prince.* London: Rider and Company, 1989.

Rutherford, Ward. *Celtic Mythology.* Wellingborough: The Aquarian Press, 1987.

Rutherford, Ward. *The Druids: Magicians of the West.* Wellingborough: The Aquarian Press, 1978.

Skinner, Stephen. *The Oracle of Geomancy.* Dorset: Prism Press, 1986.

Schwei, Priscilla, and Ralph Pestka. *The Complete Book of Astrological Geomancy.* St. Paul: Llewellyn Publications, 1990.

Stewart, R.J. *The Mystic Life of Merlin.* London: Routledge and Kegan Paul, 1986.

Thorsson, Edred. *The Book of Ogham.* St. Paul: Llewellyn Publications, 1992.

Index

On the following pages you will find listed, with their current prices, some of the books now available on related subjects. Your book dealer stocks most of these and will stock new titles in the Llewellyn series as they become available. We urge your patronage.

TO GET A FREE CATALOG

You are invited to write for our bi-monthly news magazine/catalog, *Llewellyn's New Worlds of Mind and Spirit*. A sample copy is free, and it will continue coming to you at no cost as long as you are an active mail customer. Or you may subscribe for just $10 in the United States and Canada ($20 overseas, first class mail). Many bookstores also have *New Worlds* available to their customers. Ask for it.

In *New Worlds* you will find news and features about new books, tapes and services; announcements of meetings and seminars; helpful articles; author interviews and much more. Write to:

Llewellyn's New Worlds of Mind and Spirit
P.O. Box 64383-800, St. Paul, MN 55164-0383, U.S.A.

TO ORDER BOOKS AND TAPES

If your book store does not carry the titles described on the following pages, you may order them directly from Llewellyn by sending the full price in U.S. funds, plus postage and handling (see below).

Credit card orders: VISA, MasterCard, American Express are accepted. Call us toll-free within the United States and Canada at 1-800-THE-MOON.

Special Group Discount: Because there is a great deal of interest in group discussion and study of the subject matter of this book, we offer a 20% quantity discount to group leaders or agents. Our Special Quantity Price for a minimum order of five copies of *Omens, Oghams & Oracles* is $51.80 cash-with-order. Include postage and handling charges noted below.

Postage and Handling: Include $4 postage and handling for orders $15 and under; $5 for orders *over* $15. There are no postage and handling charges for orders over $100. Postage and handling rates are subject to change. We ship UPS whenever possible within the continental United States; delivery is guaranteed. Please provide your street address as UPS does not deliver to P.O. boxes. Orders shipped to Alaska, Hawaii, Canada, Mexico and Puerto Rico will be sent via first class mail. Allow 4-6 weeks for delivery. **International orders:** Airmail – add retail price of each book and $5 for each non-book item (audiotapes, etc.); Surface mail – add $1 per item.

Minnesota residents add 7% sales tax.

Mail orders to:
Llewellyn Worldwide, P.O. Box 64383-800, St. Paul, MN 55164-0383,
U.S.A.

For customer service, call (612) 291-1970.

Prices subject to change without notice.

THE BOOK OF OGHAM
The Celtic Tree Oracle
by Edred Thorsson

Drink deeply from the very source of the Druids' traditional lore. The oghamic Celtic tradition represents an important breakthrough in the practical study of Celtic religion and magick. Within the pages of *The Book of Ogham* you will find the *complete and authentic* system of divination based on the letters of the Celtic ogham alphabet (commonly designated by tree names), and a whole world of experiential Celtic spirituality.

Come to understand the Celtic Way to new depths, discover methodological secrets shared by the Druids and Drightens of old, receive complete instructions for the practice of ogham divination, and find objective inner truths concealed deep within yourself.

The true and inner learning of oghams is a pathway to awakening the deeply rooted structural patterns of the Celtic psyche or soul. Read, study and work with the ogham oracle. . . open up the mysterious and hidden world within . . . and become part of the eternal stream of tradition that transcends the individual self. Come, and drink directly from the true cauldron of inspiration: the secret lore and practices of the ancient Celtic Druids.

0-87542-783-9, 224 pgs., 6 x 9, illus., glossary, softcover   **$12.95**

THE 21 LESSONS OF MERLYN
A Study in Druid Magic & Lore
by Douglas Monroe

For those with an inner drive to touch genuine Druidism—or who feel that the lore of King Arthur touches them personally—*The 21 Lessons of Merlyn* will come as an engrossing adventure and psychological journey into history and magic. This is a complete introductory course in Celtic Druidism, packaged within the framework of 21 authentic and expanded folk story/ lessons that read like a novel. These lessons, set in late Celtic Britain ca A.D. 500, depict the training and initiation of the real King Arthur at the hands of the real Merlyn-the-Druid: one of the last great champions of Paganism within the dawning age of Christianity. As you follow the boy Arthur's apprenticeship from his first encounter with Merlyn in the woods, you can study your own program of Druid apprentiship with the detailed practical ritual applications that follow each story. The 21 folk tales were collected by the author in Britain and Wales during a ten-year period; the Druidic teachings are based on the actual, never-before-published 16th-century manuscript entitled *The Book of Pheryllt*.

0-87542-496-1, 420 pgs., 6 x 9, illus., photos, softcover   **$12.95**

Prices subject to change without notice.

CELTIC MYTH & MAGIC
Harness the Power of the Gods & Goddesses
by Edain McCoy

Tap into the mythic power of the Celtic goddesses, gods, heroes and heroines to aid your spiritual quests and magickal goals. *Celtic Myth & Magic* explains how to use creative ritual and pathworking to align yourself with the energy of these archetypes, whose potent images live deep within your psyche.

Celtic Myth & Magic begins with an overview of 49 different types of Celtic Paganism followed today, then gives specific instructions for evoking and invoking the energy of the Celtic pantheon to channel it toward magickal and spiritual goals and into esbat, sabbat and life transition rituals. Three detailed pathworking texts will take you on an inner journey where you'll join forces with the archetypal images of Cuchulain, Queen Maeve and Merlin the Magician to bring their energies directly into your life. The last half of the book clearly details the energies of over 300 Celtic deities and mythic figures so you can evoke or invoke the appropriate deity to attain a specific goal.

This inspiring, well-researched book will help solitary Pagans who seek to expand the boundaries of their practice to form working partnerships with the divine.
1-56718-661-0, 7 x 10, 464 pp., softbound $19.95

LEGEND
The Arthurian Tarot
Anna-Marie Ferguson

Gallery artist and writer Anna-Marie Ferguson has paired the ancient divinatory system of the tarot with the Arthurian myth to create *Legend: The Arthurian Tarot*. The exquisitely beautiful watercolor paintings of this tarot deck illustrate characters, places and tales from the legends that blend traditional tarot symbolism with the Pagan and Christian symbolism that are equally significant elements of this myth.

Each card represents the Arthurian counterpart to tarot's traditional figures, such as Merlin as the Magician, Morgan le Fay as the Moon, Mordred as the King of Swords and Arthur as the Emperor. Accompanying the deck is a decorative layout sheet in the format of the Celtic Cross to inspire and guide your readings, as well as the book *Keeper of Words*, which lists the divinatory meanings of the cards, the cards' symbolism and the telling of the legend associated with each card.

The natural pairing of the tarot with Arthurian legend has been made before, but never with this much care, completeness and consummate artistry. This visionary tarot encompasses all the complex situations life has to offer—trials, challenges and rewards—to help you cultivate a close awareness of your past, present and future through the richness of the Arthurian legend ... a legend which continues to court the imagination and speak to the souls of people everywhere.

1-56718-267-4, Book: 6 x 9, 272 pgs., illus., softcover
Deck: 78 full-color cards, Layout Sheet: 18" x 24", four-color $34.95

Prices subject to change without notice.

FAERY WICCA—Book One
Theory & Magick • A Book of Shadows & Lights
Kisma Stepanich

Many books have been written on Wicca, but never until now has there been a book on the tradition of Irish Faery Wicca. If you have been drawn to the kingdom of Faery and want to gain a comprehensive understanding of this old folk faith, *Faery Wicca* offers you a thorough apprenticeship in the beliefs, history and practice of this rich and fulfilling tradition.

First, you'll explore the Irish history of Faery Wicca, its esoteric beliefs and its survival and evolution into its modern form; the Celtic pantheon; the Celtic division of the year; and the fairies of the Tuatha De Danann and their descendants. Each enlightening and informative lesson ends with a journal exercise and list of suggested readings.

The second part of *Faery Wicca* describes in detail magickal applications of the basic material presented in the first half: Faery Wicca ceremonies and rituals; utilizing magickal Faery tools, symbols and alphabets; creating sacred space; contacting and working with Faery allies; and guided visualizations and exercises suitable for beginners.

This fascinating guide will give you a firm foundation in the Faery Wicca tradition, which the upcoming *Faery Wicca, Book Two: The Shamanic Practices of Herbcraft, Spellcraft and Divination* will build upon.

1-56718-694-7, 7 x 10, 320 pp., illus., softbound $17.50

FAERY WICCA—Book Two
The Shamanic Practices of the Cunning Arts
Kisma Stepanich

Faery Wicca, Book Two is a continued study of *Faery Wicca, Book One*, with a deepening focus on the tradition's shamanic practices, including energy work, the Body Temple, healing techniques and developing Second-Sight; meditation techniques; journeys into the Otherworld; contacting Faery Guardians, Allies, Guides and Companions; herbcraft and spellcasting; different forms of Faery divination; rites of passages; the four minor holidays; and a closing statement on the shamanic technique known as "remembering."

The Oral Faery Tradition's teachings are not about little winged creatures. They are about the primal earth and the power therein, the circles of existence, Ancient Gods, the ancestors and the continuum. *Faery Wicca, Book Two* is not a how-to book but a study that provides extensive background information and mystery teachings for both novices and adepts alike.

1-56718-695-5, 7 x 10, 320 pp., illus., softbound $17.50

Prices subject to change without notice.

THE SACRED CAULDRON
Secrets of the Druids
by Tadhg MacCrossan

Here is a comprehensive course in the history and development of Celtic religious lore, the secrets taught by the Druids, and a guide to the modern performance of the rites and ceremonies as practiced by members of the "Druidactos," a spiritual organization devoted to the revival of this ancient way of life.

The Sacred Cauldron evolved out of MacCrossan's extensive research in comparative mythology and Indo-European linguistics, etymology and archaeology. He has gone beyond the stereotypical image of standing stones and white-robed priests to piece together the truth about Druidism. The reader will find detailed interpretations of the words, phrases and titles that are indigenous to this ancient religion. Here also are step-by-step instructions for ceremonial rites for modern-day practice.

0-87542-103-2, 302 pgs., 5¼ x 8, illus., softcover $10.95

THE CRAFTED CUP
Ritual Mysteries of the Goddess and the Grail
by Shadwynn

The Holy Grail—fabled depository of wonder, enchantment and ultimate spiritual fulfillment—is the key by which the wellsprings of a Deeper Life can be tapped for the enhancement of our inner growth. *The Crafted Cup* is a compendium of the teachings and rituals of a distinctly Pagan religious Order—the *Ordo Arcanorum Gradalis*—which incorporates into its spiritual way of worship ritual imagery based upon the Arthurian Grail legends, a reverence towards the mythic Christ, and an appreciation of the core truths and techniques found scattered throughout the New Age movement.

The Crafted Cup is divided into two parts. The first deals specifically with the teachings and general concepts which hold a central place within the philosophy of the *Ordo Arcanorum Gradalis*. The second and larger of the two parts is a complete compilation of the sacramental rites and seasonal rituals which make up the liturgical calendar of the Order. It contains one of the largest collections of Pagan, Grail-oriented rituals yet published.

0-87542-739-1, 420 pgs., 7 X 10, illus., softcover $19.95

Prices subject to change without notice.

CELTIC MAGIC
by D. J. Conway

Many people, not all of Irish descent, have a great interest in the ancient Celts and the Celtic pantheon, and *Celtic Magic* is the map they need for exploring this ancient and fascinating magical culture.

Celtic Magic is for the reader who is either a beginner or intermediate in the field of magic. It provides an extensive "how-to" of practical spell-working. There are many books on the market dealing with the Celts and their beliefs, but none guide the reader to a practical application of magical knowledge for use in everyday life. There is also an in-depth discussion of Celtic deities and the Celtic way of life and worship, so that an intermediate practitioner can expand upon the spellwork to build a series of magical rituals. Presented in an easy-to-understand format, *Celtic Magic* is for anyone searching for new spells that can be worked immediately, without elaborate or rare materials, and with minimal time and preparation.

0-87542-136-9, 240 pgs., mass market, illus.   **$3.95**

THE HANDBOOK OF CELTIC ASTROLOGY
The 13-Sign Lunar Zodiac of the Ancient Druids
Helena Paterson

Discover your lunar self with *The Handbook of Celtic Astrology!* Solar-oriented astrology has dominated Western astrological thought for centuries, but lunar-based Celtic astrology provides the "Yin" principle that has been neglected in the West—and author Helena Paterson presents new concepts based on ancient Druidic observations, lore and traditions that will redefine Western astrology.

This reference work will take you through the Celtic lunar zodiac, where each lunar month is associated with one of the 13 trees sacred to the Druids: birch, rowan, ash, alder, willow, hawthorn, oak, holly, hazel, vine, ivy, reed and elder. Chapters on each "tree sign" provide comprehensive text on Celtic mythology and gods/desses associated with the sign's ruling tree and planet; general characteristics of natives of the sign; and interpretive notes on the locations of the planets, the Moon, the ascendant and Midheaven as they are placed in any of the three decans of each tree sign. A thorough introduction on chart construction, sign division and the importance of solstices, equinoxes, eclipses and aspects to the Moon guarantees this book will become *the* definitive work on Celtic astrology.

1-56718-509-6, 7 x 10, 288 pp., illus.   **$15.00**

THE CELTIC HEART
Kathryn Marie Cocquyt

The Celtic Heart tells the adventurous, epic tale of spirit, love, loss, and the difficult choices made by three generations of the Celtic Brigantes tribe, who once lived off the coast of North Wales on an island they named *Mona mam Cymru* ("Mother of Wales," or Anglesey).

Follow the passionate lives of the Brigantes clan and the tumultuous events during the years leading up to the Roman Invasion in A.D. 61, when Anglesey was a refuge for Celts struggling to preserve their inner truths and goddess-based culture against the encroachment of the Roman Empire and Christianity. As their tribal way of life is threatened, the courageous natures of the Chieftain Solomon, the Druidess Saturnalia, and the young warriors Kordelina and Aonghus are tested by the same questions of good and evil that face us today.

Filled with ritual, dream images, romance, and intrigue, *The Celtic Heart* will take you on an authentic and absorbing journey into the history, lives, and hearts of the legendary Celts.
1-56718-156-2, 6 x 9, 624 pp., softbound   **$14.95**

DANCING WITH DRAGONS
Invoke Their Ageless Wisdom & Power
D. J. Conway

You can access one of the most potent life forces in the astral universe: the wise and magickal dragon. Dragons *do* exist! They inhabit the astral plane that interpenetrates our physical world. Now, *Dancing with Dragons* makes a vast and wonderful hoard of dragon magick and power available to you.

Dancing with Dragons is a ritual textbook that will teach you to call, befriend, and utilize the wisdom of these powerful mythical creatures for increased spiritual fulfillment, knowledge, health, and happiness. Here you will find complete, practical information for working with dragons: spells and rituals ranging from simple to advanced workings; designing ritual tools to aid you in using dragon energy; channeling power using the lines of dragon's breath (energy lines that run through the Earth); and using the true language of dragons in ritual and spell-casting with herbs, oils, stones, and candles.

Dancing with dragons is a joyful experience. Whether you are a practicing magician, a devotee of role-playing games, or a seeker who wishes to tap the dragon's vast astral power, this book will help you forge a friendship and magickal partnership with these astral creatures.
1-56718-165-1, 7 x 10 • 320 pp., illus., softbound   **$14.95**

Prices subject to change without notice.